Welcome to the Departure Lounge

Welcome to the Departure Lounge

Adventures in Mothering Mother

Meg Federico

Random House New York

Published in the United States by Random House,
an imprint of The Random House Publishing Group,
a division of Random House, Inc., New York.

ISBN: 978-1-4000-6795-4

Printed in the United States of America on acid-free paper

www.atrandom.com

1 2 3 4 5 6 7 8 9

First Edition

Book design by Susan Turner

This book is dedicated to those we take care of, and to those who take care of us; to the memory of my mother, without whom my life would not have been.

Contents

A Note to the Reader

Welcome to the Departure Lounge is a memoir written over the course of ten years. I have relied on my own observations and memories, though a few stories were reported to me. I have taken the liberty of shaping the scribbled accounts in my journal into a narrative. Unavoidably, the contributions of my brothers and sisters, additional relatives, and friends to the care of my mother and stepfather are not fully reflected in my rendering, and some events have been simplified in service of clarity.

Further, to avoid identifying details, I changed names and identifying details for people, names for most businesses and institutions, and names for some locations. The location Greystone Gallery, in chapter 7 ("To Her Health"), is a fictionalized composite, drawn from my memory of several galleries patronized by my mother over the course of many years.

And I'd like to acknowledge that for many family caregivers, coming up with the money to provide for aging parents is a crippling concern.

Meg Federico

Welcome to the Departure Lounge

Chapter One

I DEMAND AN AUTOPSY!

I was sitting at my desk plowing through bills when the phone rang. My stepsister, Cathy, never called unless we had "problems." Her father, Walter Huber (age eighty-two), and my mother, Addie Henry (age eighty-one), after a dramatic and sometimes bruising courtship, married a few years ago. Not one of the eight offspring (me and my four siblings, Cathy and her two) in our newly blended family was pleased about this union, but there was nothing we could do about it. After all, our parents were grown-ups.

At present, Addie and Walter were escaping the New Jersey winter, vacationing in West Palm Beach, Florida, where, Cathy informed me, Mom stumbled and fell and hit her head on the curb. A stranger, seeing the two old people in a state of emergency (a fairly common sight in Florida), kindly called an ambulance for Mom and packed Walter into a taxi.

The ambulance paramedic, recoiling from Mother's ninety-proof breath, scribbled *ETOH* all over her medical forms. *ETOH* is medical jargon for ethanol. In Mom's case, it meant martinis.

While Mom was out cold, the ER staff tried to pry information out of Walter, who was upset and couldn't remember anything. Suddenly, Mom sat bolt upright on the gurney and yelled, "I demand an autopsy!" before passing out again.

"I'm not getting an autopsy!" Walter roared. "You have to be *dead* to get an autopsy!" Apparently, after the nurses got him calmed down, they shipped him off to an emergency Alzheimer's unit (which they also have in Florida), where he had been locked up for three days before he finally divulged Cathy's number. She was now on her way to retrieve him.

I called St. Stephen's Hospital and finally got Mom. "Oh, hello, dearie," she said brightly, as though I just happened to call as she bounded off the tennis court. "Isn't this a bore? I could leave right now, but to be safe I thought I'd get a few tests done." She sounded peachy. "A lamp fell on my head at the hotel, but really it's nothing. A big old Biedermeier lamp!" Like any good liar, she added the Biedermeier bit to make her story plausible. The facts were irrelevant; I wasn't going to win any arguments against that lamp.

Watching my mother for the past few years had been a lot like watching a blindfolded lady ride a unicycle on a tightrope. You can't take your eyes off her as she wobbles up there completely unaware that she's fifty feet above the ground because she can't see. And if you attempt to point out her peril, she thinks you're trying to ruin her career. Just when you're sure she's going to plunge to her death, the blind lady yanks the bike upright. "See?" she says. "You worry too much."

I did worry. I'd been worried for years, because one day Mom was going to fall. It would be a terrible accident I could not prevent, and she might just fall right on top of *me*.

Then later that same day, Cathy called again, from the Sunshine State. Our problems were getting worse. "You better get down here. This hospital is not exactly Columbia-Presbyterian, and frankly I have my hands full with Walter." The emergency lockup ward for stray dementia folks was like a holding cell. Walter's suitcase had been ransacked and his wallet emptied, and he was so distraught he'd forgotten how to use the toilet.

"The food here isn't as good as the other places," he confided to Cathy, presumably referring to the swanky four-star resorts he and Mom patronized. "And that fellow is not very interesting," he said, indicating his roommate, who could only burble.

I lived in Nova Scotia, a thousand miles from Mom's house in New Jersey and a lot farther than that from West Palm Beach. I had a job (fund-raising), three children (a son, fourteen; two daughters, twelve and eleven), a husband (Rob), and a dog. My mother was going blind, and as she gradually lost her eyesight she began to drink even more heavily than she had before. Sometimes Walter drove her to the ER, where she got stitched up and was kept overnight for observation. Sometimes an ambulance was required.

I rarely heard about these accidents from Mom because she didn't want me to know. One of her remaining gossipy friends would report the gory details of each debacle with keen enthusiasm.

"I'm glad your father didn't live long enough to see this!" declared my informant.

I didn't bother to point out that if Daddy weren't planted in the family plot, Mom would not be running around with Walter.

If the situation sounded bad enough, I jumped on a plane. But it had to be sufficiently dire to warrant the turmoil: getting time off work, lining up babysitters, convincing my skeptical spouse we had to spend the money. Of course, it's very hard to tell, long-distance, how bad things really are. My half sister, Alice, lived in New Jersey not that far from Addie, but I hated to ask Alice to shoulder Addie's predicaments. (Alice had recently dealt with her own mother's illness and death—she'd fulfilled *her* filial duties.) My brothers and my sister all lived a plane ride away; we had to jump through hoops and pass through time zones to get back home. I was usually the first responder on the crisis management team because my flight was the shortest.

But back to West Palm Beach. First the good news: Walter was diagnosed with Alzheimer's disease. That he had it wasn't good, but finally a *doctor* had said so. Frankly, I'd always found Walter scary. One minute he was calling Mom his "beloved Bride," the next he was shaking his fist at her, red-faced and swearing. If I was around, he'd yell at me, too. And he drove on the wrong side of the road. When I tried to talk to Cathy about him, I got nowhere. "He's always been like that," she'd say. I naïvely thought that an expert medical diagnosis would change things for the better. Now, instead of running around loose, Walter would be managed. By experts.

The bad news was that over the course of the next few days, my mother went from her bossy self to an "unresponsive state," and the hospital offered no explanation. I hit the phone lines and frantically briefed my brothers and sisters, choreographed a quick departure (babysitter, dog walker, tuna noodle casserole), and got on a plane. As the jet thundered down the runway, I had no idea if, on the return trip, I'd be drinking martinis with Mom in executive class or accompanying her home in a box.

I had a five-hour layover in the Continental terminal at Newark Airport, which is not my favorite place because years ago, quite possibly in the exact spot where I sat waiting for my flight to West Palm Beach, my father dropped dead of a heart attack. I was getting married and on the day before my wedding, my oldest brother, William, was flying in for the big event. Dad invited me along for the ride out to the airport, but I didn't want to get stuck in the backseat of the Buick while he drove Mom crazy by telling her how to drive. The whole reason *she* was driving in the first place was that Dad couldn't see an elephant if it was seated on the dashboard. On the other hand, Mom was so accustomed to his insistent navigation, she couldn't get anywhere without him: Dad hunching forward in his seat telling her to watch the road, Mother sighing dramatically to let him know she was just *letting* him *think* she was taking orders—I couldn't stand it.

So I told Dad I had a few last-minute bride-type errands—and while Dad was dying, I was in a department store buying a beige slip.

When my stupid errand was finished, I sat drinking tea in the kitchen with Frances, the black lady who had pretty much raised me. She fiddled with cut flowers for the guest rooms, humming, "Loh de doh," under her breath, as she had for as long as I could remember. I hummed that song myself sometimes: *Loh de doh*. "They must have hit traffic," I said to Frances.

Then William called to say that Dad had had a heart attack. Airports have defibrillators stationed all over the place now, but twenty years ago they did not.

"It doesn't look good, honey," he said from a pay phone.

For years, Dad had never gone out of the house without a vial of nitro tablets in his pocket, but in the end they didn't save him. Who knows if he even had time to get one into his mouth? I thought of him hurrying down the concourse with his crookedy old-man walk and then falling, collapsing, while people like me looked on.

Maybe those people still tell the story about the time they saw the old man drop dead in the airport.

My mother didn't miss a beat. By the next morning she had a huge mess on her hands because cases of wedding champagne were being delivered at the back door, as the first of the funeral flowers were arriving at the front. Confronting the real disaster—namely, life without Dad—would have to wait. The rest of us could afford to go numb, but Mom had to move into action.

She stationed herself in the dining room with a yellow legal pad and a very sharp pencil, her blouse crisp, the stiff collar framing her face. The platinum wedding band on her finger looked obvious and sad. As I slid into a chair, Frances placed a hot cup of coffee in front of me. We didn't say a word to each other, because those were the dining room rules.

Mom tapped her pencil and frowned at her long list. She must have figured that Dad would die first; he was so much older than she was. She had probably planned the funeral years ago or at least thought about it, because she was big on planning ahead. Looking up at me, she jumped right in.

"Darling, your father's favorite suit, the blue pinstripe he wanted to wear to your wedding? It's fresh from the dry cleaner. Would you mind, terribly, if he was buried in that suit?"

"Of course not, Mother."

"Now, the dress I was going to wear to the wedding is navy and it isn't low-cut, really. It's just as appropriate for a funeral, so would you mind if I—"

"Of course not," I said. Mother gripped her pencil with both hands, before releasing it to target another item.

"Darling, the wedding caterers? Well, I asked them to handle the funeral reception. They're all set to make the tortellini and the—"

"That will be fine," I said, as she checked that item off her list.

"And if we slice it in the kitchen and serve it directly on plates, no one will recognize the wedding cake."

I gulped. I did not want those mourners eating what they thought was just some nice white cake! My father was dead and my wedding was canceled. I wanted to stand on a cliff and throw the cake—all three layers, plus the plastic bride and groom—into the ocean while everyone watched and felt sorry for me.

"Of course you can, Mom," I said.

"About your wedding, dear—it's terrible. Your father would be so distressed about it, if he knew." Mother gazed at me tenderly, and I felt the tears well up. "But it is really *so* convenient that everyone is already on their way. Saves a lot of phone calls." I choked on my coffee.

Within a day, the entire event had been transformed from wedding white to bereavement black, with the exception of one small detail. I couldn't reach the wedding photographer, who was probably out taking pictures of some other bride and groom, who'd never know how lucky they were.

"*Candid Shots of Dad's Funeral* will look nice on your coffee table," said William as he chewed on a slice of ham. Funeral hams were now arriving along with the flowers, and Mom sent the champagne back. "Tasteful black leather, gold lettering, and the date—now, wouldn't that be a conversation piece?" he asked through another large mouthful. In our family, everyone eats and makes wisecracks rather than messy displays of grief.

"That is not funny," I told him, but I laughed.

Of course there is no such album, because I managed to cancel the photographer at the last minute. Then, figuring there was no point in waiting, Rob and I ran down to City Hall and got married. In lieu of a celebration, my entire extended family—all seventeen of us—descended on Black's funeral home.

Every room in the converted Victorian house displayed caskets, discreetly backlit and adorned with real flowers. Gleaming wood and polished brass created a corporate atmosphere. We chose the "Executive," which seemed fitting for the businessman my father had been. On the day of his viewing, dressed as though ready for a day at work, he looked a lot like he was lying in a large desk drawer.

The grandchildren feigned terror at the sight of a dead body, but poked at Dad's face when no one was looking, then climbed underneath the coffin, where they played comfortably out of the way in a world of their own.

The reception after the burial was crowded and noisy. People juggled their drinks and plates of tortellini, salad spilling over the edge. But Mom stood in her navy-blue dress, smiling and nodding with a polite disinterest that deflected the slightest intimacy. Without Dad, Mom was stranded. Once or twice I saw her eye the crowd, exasperation crossing her face: *Now, where has he gotten to?* Then she remembered, and her shoulders sagged. A gloss of manners and poise held her together so effectively that my cousin thought Mom didn't care. But, to me, those sagging shoulders said it all.

And poor Rob—as he ate his incognito wedding cake, people kept pumping his hand, saying, "Congratulations, we're so sorry."

Now I wish I had a few photos. Just one or two.

Frankly, there are some events that you simply cannot be prepared for—and this trip to Florida would soon prove to be one of them. When I landed in West Palm Beach, my luggage did not. I stepped into the warm, balmy air with nothing but the clothes on my back. I should have seen it as an omen. Losing my belongings would be nothing compared to the chaos of the next few weeks.

When I got off the hospital elevator, a nurse stood staring at the floor, while a doctor waved a chart in her face yelling, "After he got stitched up, he was supposed to go back to jail!" Dirty linens piled up in the corners, garbage cans overflowed, stacks of charts at the nursing station threatened to collapse. Families crowded around doorways, straining to see the relative on the bed. A young woman in a blue uniform dragged a laundry bin behind her, bumping into walls. A teenager pushed past her on a skateboard. Phones rang, monitors beeped, and televisions gabbled.

Mom was prone and immobile on a hospital bed crammed into a tiny room. Her face, collapsed in sleep, was unnaturally yellow from the disinfectant slopped over a blue-and-brown bruise that spread from her jawline past her ear, as though she'd gone down in a bar fight. I was dumbstruck at the sight of her, so broken and diminished. I lifted her hand to my cheek. Her nails, always filed and buffed, were dirty. In such a state of neglect, who would want to recover? I'd go into a coma, too.

Like Diana, the "People's Princess," Addie was the "People's Aristocrat," at least as far as the town of Oldhill, New Jersey, was concerned. When Addie arrived, tidy and tasteful in her alligator pumps, a silk scarf knotted at the collar of her sensible camel-hair coat, everyone from the gas station man to the bank president perked up. Her propriety, tempered with a conspiratorial twinkle, gave people a lift as she said her "How do you do"'s. Wherever she went, a murmur of appreciation followed.

"Your mother is such a lady," people said. "Real class."

The slit of a window let in the Florida sun, illuminating a couple of Trollope novels and a technical book on archaeology on the windowsill. Mom never traveled without her books. When she was younger, a whole suitcase had been dedicated to her vacation reading. Within the family, of course, the People's Aristocrat was harder to take, determined as she was to make us all into aristocrats, not to mention intellectuals, by insisting on strict codes of etiquette and comportment and a stiff reading requirement: a book per week or no TV.

The figure on the bed was not my brilliant, beautiful, know-it-all mother. This was vegetable Mom, who might never recognize—or contradict—me again. I shook her gently by the shoulder, but she was way down deep, beyond my tears. I sat looking at her for a long time.

Finally, I took a little walk down the hall and located the supply closet. No one noticed as I commandeered a mop, bucket, sponges, and rubber gloves. I dusted, scrubbed, and scoured Mom's room, as if by exorcising this tiny bit of territory I could get some kind of meaningful grip. I stopped periodically to look at Mom, but she remained unchanged and unreachable.

"They paying you to work here already?" said a familiar voice. William stood in the doorway holding a grocery bag, a cardboard tube, and flowers. He was a remarkable sight even to me, his little sister. Dressed in red boxing shoes, leather pants, a white formal shirt, and a silver-and-black-striped tie, he had a baseball hat pulled down over his eyes, and his skin had the purple cast people get when they spend too much time on airplanes. The mop clattered to the floor as I threw my arms around him.

William is ten years older than I am. By the time I was five, he was being shipped off to camp in summer and boarding school the rest of the time, so I grew up without him. But one Christmas when I was a teenager, he caught me smoking a joint. The bathroom was filled with smoke as I anesthetized myself against the annual Christmas Eve party. The baked lasagna, the aunts and uncles bellowing "Good King Wenceslas," and my cousin playing the tuba—it was all too much to bear. When William busted me, I was terrified until he said, "Give me that or I'll tell. And put another towel under the door."

Like Mom, William knows everything about everything and is very generous with his opinions. He writes poetry, mysteries, and opera librettos, which makes him an endangered species. He is serious about cooking, eating, culture, and girlfriends, and he is ultimately sympathetic even to his enemies, which might explain why all his ex-girlfriends once got together and threw him a party.

"I've been trying to find a doctor. Any doctor," he said, sticking a bouquet of yellow chrysanthemums and blue freesia into the water pitcher and dumping oranges into the plastic throw-up bowl. He pulled a poster of Seurat's "Sunday in the Park" painting out of the tube and taped it to the wall. "I never liked these people," he said, regarding figures so stiff they couldn't possibly be enjoying themselves, not even the dog. "But I didn't have a choice; it was either them or *The Scream.*"

The atmosphere was much improved. If Mother woke up, she might feel like living. William plopped down on the bed. "Hi, Mom," he said, leaning over her. "How're you doing?" Mom blew little frothy bubbles and snored. "You don't say," he said, patting her. "I'm pretending you can hear me."

He unwrapped a turkey sandwich and handed me half. "All I know is, one minute she's commanding the troops as usual and the next time I tune in for a report—this. The nursing notes are illegible and the doctors have vanished. I can't find out what's wrong with her."

Mom looked peaceful, as peaceful as a baby. Then a little frown crossed her face, followed a moment later by a very bad smell. I sniffed and gagged before I connected the dots. William and I turned to each other, horrified.

"Mother, how could you?" William said. "How indiscreet." Mom wheezed gently.

I hit the call button. When no one showed up, William went in search of help and returned with bad news. "There's only one guy on the floor, and he can't get over here." We waited for a while, then waited some more. It was a very busy afternoon out there—heart attacks, uncontrollable bleeding, a knife fight between a man and his wife's ex-husband. We had no choice but to clean up Mom ourselves. "Come on, you've raised kids and I've had puppies," William said, and we plunged in.

I'd never considered the mechanics of changing a grown-up's diaper, and I'd certainly never thought I'd get my first chance on Mother. It was a good thing she was oblivious because William and I were clueless. Somehow we bumbled through the exercise without dropping her on the floor.

A lifetime later, Mom lay pristine in her bed, breathing in and breathing out, unknowing. My brother slumped on the chair in front of me, his elbows on his knees and his chin in his hands. We had exhausted our bravado. "Well, I hope they aren't feeding her prunes," he said. When we were growing up, we were often confronted at breakfast by little glass dishes of nasty prunes that Mother forced us to eat. She was obsessed with our bowel movements. Now it looked like we were going to become obsessed with hers. William rubbed his face. "We have got to get her out of here. I don't want to make a career out of this."

But it didn't take long before coping with Mom *did* begin to look like a career—I kept meeting new people: nurses, physical therapists, a guy who made his living renting out wheelchairs. I couldn't remember who said what without taking notes, and I ended up with a collection of barely legible scraps. But at least I had those, because people who did not seem relevant at the time turned out to be a big help later on. I managed to capture the name and number for almost every smiling or frowning face. William, Addie, and I were in uncharted waters and who knew when we might need a favor. So I made a point of thanking every person I met, like a store credit I might need to cash in later.

This was not the glamorous part of West Palm Beach. The shopping centers, hotels, nursing homes, and funeral parlors were all the same: three-story white buildings with parking lots. This was the authentic part of town, the slummy section just before the hospital, with Rottweilers chained in yards, laundry on the line, and men sitting on stoops midmorning, smoking and shooting the breeze.

William and I got Hershey bars and notebooks at a candy store that also sold guns and pictures of Jesus. Any problem, regardless of complexity or magnitude, would fit in that notebook. The simple act of writing my name and phone number on the front cover cheered me up.

William and I moved into a motel located directly behind Rebecca's Naked Ladies nightclub, which, we were told, was famous for strip sirloin. We sat around a little chlorinated pool in the dark, ate pizza, and watched beetles and moths fly into a big blue zapper while we invented elaborate schemes to get Mom back to New Jersey, dead or alive. We could do nothing but speculate because we had no facts. You naïvely believe you'll be able to make good, sound decisions if you can just get the facts.

While I was sleeping on my board-like motel bed, Penny, a tiny Filipino nurse, had been up all night with Mom. In the morning, she intercepted William and me in the corridor. "Four A.M. she want ice cream. She want go home. She get out of bed and head for door."

"So I take it she woke up," said William.

"She plenty awake." Penny energetically propelled us forward.

Mother was tied to the bed in a Posey, a restraint device akin to a straitjacket. She smiled wildly, propped upright on a stack of pillows.

"Ha! Ha!" Penny said. "See. We brush hair. So pretty. We put on lipstick." Mom was electrified. Her eyes were all lit up and flashing. Her hair, full of static, flew around her head, and her mouth was bright red and smeared.

"Ha! Ha!" Mother crowed, imitating Penny, her eyes glittering as she swiveled her head from side to side like a bird. "Purse, purse. *Purse!*" She glared at William, who, undone by Mother's disturbing transformation, backed toward the door.

"You be good, Mommy. Stay in bed," Penny said. Mom, suddenly as docile as a bunny, gave her an obedient smile. "I take Posey off if you watch her," Penny said to us. Like fools, we nodded in unison.

Penny untied the Posey while I rummaged around in the closet and found Mother's small black patent-leather purse. She snatched it and dug through the contents, finding her wallet and waving it around, scattering credit cards on the floor.

"How is the man up there?" Mom asked William as she pointed to the ceiling.

"Quite well, as far as I know," William said.

"I shot him in the head." Then she dropped her purse and began picking at the sheets. "Tell the caterer there will be fifty of us for lunch." The way she said "for lunch" was distinctly Katharine Hepburn's "fah lanch."

"And tell that man I'll shoot him again. Where has he gone to?"

"Boy," William said, "where are the Marx Brothers when we need them?"

"The limo is ready—hurry hurry!" Mom thrashed around in the bed, trying to get up.

"No, no, honey!" yelled Penny. "You stay in bed. You be good mommy."

"High heels, black hat!" yelled Mother, straining, her hands outstretched toward the closet. "Lincoln Tunnel!" Penny put one hand on Mom's chest and expertly retied the Posey. Mother rolled back and forth, cackling and hooting. William and I were so unnerved, we bolted.

We fled to the smoking lounge, an airless, windowless dump in the hospital basement, patronized exclusively by cancer patients and doctors. With cigarettes wagging in their mouths, these doctors did not resemble their counterparts on daytime TV. One with shaggy hair and a beard looked an awful lot like Doctor Moreau.

"Do you think Mom will stay like this?" I asked William as he lit a cigarette.

"One minute she is unconscious, the next she's nuts. So who knows?"

"Those doctors—that's who knows," I hissed, pointing in what was, I hoped, a covert fashion. But before we had worked up the gumption to corner them, they stubbed their cigarettes out in the bucket of sand provided, and slithered off through the doors.

"One of those learned colleagues has to start talking to us," said William, mimicking Mother's loony laugh. "Ha! Ha!"

The company that owned St. Stephen's Hospital was trying to shut it down. The clientele—guys from jail and poverty-ridden inner-city families with no health insurance—were bankrupting the operation. A recent court order was forcing the hospital to remain open, but the doctors were rarely on site. The hospital was run by nurses, orderlies, and security guards, none of whom knew anything about Mom.

I started walking into offices introducing myself, asking for help, scribbling in my notebook, and learning that when they give you a business card, they're trying to get rid of you. Wandering the corridors, I finally found a social worker who thought Mom had been discharged the day before. "I'll get right on it for you," she said. "How long will you be here?"

I'd told my husband I'd be gone for about a week, which had seemed long enough to deal with anything, even a funeral. But now, I had no idea. "Well, I guess I'll be here until Mom goes home," I said, not knowing when that would be.

Cathy, meanwhile, had gotten Walter out of the Alzheimer's joint and had flown him back to New Jersey. Now, in addition to *her* kids, husband, job, and dog, Cathy also had to worry about Walter, who could not be left to care for himself. For years, Mother had been covering for him, just barely, but those days were over.

"Where's my Bride?" he asked Cathy repeatedly.

"She's in the hospital, Dad. She had an accident."

"She did? Nobody told me!" Walter and Cathy had this conversation for weeks.

Mother, meanwhile, was getting worse. "Where are my slaves?" she yelled at the nurses and orderlies, mostly people of color.

"You really cannot say that!" I whispered forcefully. Mom may have harbored some rather snobby ideas about class and breeding, but she was not a racist. When I was a girl, she took me to hear Martin Luther King, Jr., knowing how important he was, knowing we would be the only white people in the church.

"Slaves!" she yelled, louder. Mom depended on decorum (even when she was drinking), and part of her knew her behavior was anything but decorous as she wet the bed, clawed at the orderlies, and screamed mean, hurtful things. More than once, I locked myself in the bathroom and cried, for all of us, because it was so sad.

On a good day, we had silly conversations to the tune of A. A. Milne. "Here comes nursey nursey nursey!" Mom said.

"Bringing your coffee coffee coffee," I said.

"Happy happy happy!" Mom sang.

The weird thing was, I kind of liked her this way. She was nutty, which was very disturbing, but she was also warm and simple. Ordinarily, my mother was so damn complicated, anything she said required decoding. But this mom was vulnerable, crazy, and available. "You're my honey bunny one-y," she crowed and, absurdly, I swelled up with happiness as if my addlepated mother actually meant it. The sweetness was heartbreaking. I hated to leave her for even a minute.

The situation wasn't moving forward. The orderlies didn't bother to clean Mom's room because we were doing it. One lady, thinking I worked there, asked me to clean her mother's room as well. I showed her where the supply closet was and told her to help herself. And we kept waiting for doctors who did not show up.

"Mommy, come home!" my daughter sobbed on the phone. She hated the babysitter, whose enthusiasm for my family had waned with each extra day of duty.

"What about us?" asked Rob, his padding and insulation wearing thin. A week had gone by with no end in sight. "Can't you hire someone to look after Addie? She can afford it more than we can afford this useless babysitter!"

My boss, at the end of her rope, said, "We really need to talk."

If I packed up and left, I was a bad daughter; if I stayed, I was a bad mother. But, for me, bad-daughter guilt trumped bad-mom-spouse guilt. Practically speaking, I had plenty of time to make up for being a bad mom, but with the sand running out of the hourglass, hardly any time left to be a good daughter. I told myself the kids would survive. I told Rob I had no choice, and neither did he.

After days of no-show doctors and no plan, it dawned on me that we could hang around cleaning Mom's room and meeting interesting people like Penny forever. As long as Mom's insurance was paying, no one was going to hand us an exit strategy. We had to make it happen.

"You go after the floor staff," I told William. "I'll tackle the doctors."

I borrowed William's cigarettes and went in search of those shy, elusive creatures in the smoking lounge. The scary one with the beard was Mom's neurologist. I batted my eyes at him and pretended to smoke.

Mom's neurologist, it turned out, had fled to Florida after being hounded by malpractice suits in Connecticut. His wife got custody of the kids. "Now I'm paying a divorce lawyer, too," he complained, like the most dejected man on earth. Malpractice or not, he was my only hope. I poured on the sympathy, and he promised me a CAT scan and his pager number. When we parted, he squeezed my hand and said, "Call me Peter."

The other doctors were harder to catch. I lay in ambush outside the men's room and loitered in the coffee shop. But even after three separate coffee dates, the wall-eyed trauma doctor wouldn't give me a straight answer. I was convinced Mom had had a stroke, but he wouldn't support my diagnosis for fear of getting sued—if he hadn't been already. Eventually we made a deal: While not saying the word *stroke,* we agreed she had a big pool of blood sloshing around in her head, swelling and putting pressure on her brain and clotting. Her craziness was partially from this trauma and partially from alcohol abuse. If she didn't drink and didn't fall, Mom might, over time, recover.

With the determination of a field general, William captured the real power brokers: the nurses, social workers, and secretaries. Flowers arrived at the nurses' station. Pizza and sushi materialized in the staff lounge. A huge box of cookies in Mom's room pulled in the orderlies. William gave the social worker a box of chocolates, and a fifty-dollar phone card went to Penny.

Mother's room turned into the social hot spot, and she got plenty of attention as a result. The windows sparkled, the floor gleamed, and many extra pillows, towels, and pitchers of ice water showed up.

In a day, we knew everyone's life story. Donna was a single parent, trying to upgrade her nursing skills. Billy was part Sioux and had traveled all over the country, working his way from city to city through the ERs and sending money home to his mom. Penny, who lived with eleven children and two grandchildren in a three-bedroom apartment, was putting her oldest son through college. Helen, an orderly, worked three jobs while her husband was in detox, again: "I think he might make it this time."

Hospitals are full of the wounded and the damaged, and plenty of them just *work* there.

The plan was to get Mom admitted to Brookside Hospital in New Jersey. On our end, we'd hound our hospital in Florida for a discharge. Alice agreed to hound the hospital there, pulling every string she could. The paperwork was overwhelming. Signatures were required from all the doctors at St. Stephen's who had so much as walked past Mom's door. After chasing them from floor to floor to no avail, I was tempted to grab the microphone at the nursing station and page them myself.

We needed a doctor in New Jersey who'd "accept delivery" to get her into the hospital there, but we couldn't contact her beloved doctor—he was on vacation in *Florida*—so we got one out of the Yellow Pages. Finally, after we ran around both hospitals day and night with clipboards and pens, all arrangements were complete.

Mom had to travel lying down, so we rented a medical transport jet (also from the Yellow Pages) and charged it to her American Express card. William looked through Mom's suitcase and discovered a wrinkled skirt and blouse, which he deemed inadequate garb for invalid air travel. "Something concealing and dignified," he said as I accompanied him to Dillard's, a large, upscale department store. Within moments we found ourselves adrift in an entire floor of lingerie.

The Large and Luscious Women's Collection (for the far end of the alphabet) featured steel-cable engineering that rivaled the Brooklyn Bridge. These support garments did not cringe in beige; they confronted us in neon pink, purple, and green, and were more suggestive than a gymnastic troupe of naked women.

William was mortified. He had never been exposed to this side of the feminine mystique, which inexplicably embarrassed him more than changing his mother's diapers. We escaped to the monochromatic men's department, where we bought Mom a black velour bathrobe from a nice bland man in a toupee.

The day of our departure, Mom rejected the bathrobe in favor of the wrinkled skirt and insisted on panty hose. Getting her into those was a lot like dressing a cat, but if panty hose would ensure her compliance, I was willing. She also demanded her black straw hat, suitable for tea with the Queen. We were a sight: me in my stained and ragged clothes; William resplendent in baseball hat, sunglasses, and white aviator's scarf; and Mom wrapped up like a mummy, wearing a hat, and strapped to a gurney.

After almost three weeks, the days of fresh flowers and phone cards were over for our friends at the hospital, who were sad to see us go. William had broken a few hearts among the nurses, and I was relieved I hadn't had to date Dr. Peter.

As I strapped myself into the luxurious leather seat of our own private plane, relief made me weak. Bye-bye, palm trees. So long, alligators. As the little jet shot into the sky, the flight nurse checked Mom's blood pressure and then, because she was also the stewardess, served drinks and little sandwiches on a silver plastic tray, like we were at some weird office party. The feeling onboard was almost festive. We thought that at last we were getting somewhere.

You won't be surprised to learn the jet's altimeter broke over Virginia, requiring us to return to a tiny Florida landing strip, where we sat sweating in a seedy Quonset hut, thumbing through greasy issues of *Aeromarkt* magazine to pass four or so hours. Since she couldn't sit up, Mother remained unglamorously tied to the transfer bed, her big black hat squashed flat. The pilot loitered around the nurse-stewardess, whispering and winking. Finally, a replacement jet arrived, bearing more festive sandwiches. Once again, as we thundered into the sky, I mistook momentum for progress.

Upon our dismal midnight arrival at Brookside Hospital, we were greeted by Alice, who had waited faithfully, pacing back and forth in her wrinkled raincoat and clutching Mom's admission papers, and a private duty nurse, thoughtfully hired by Cathy.

Alice gave me a forlorn embrace, batting me accidentally with the file. "I was afraid that if I let anyone else touch your mother's documents, they'd be forever lost in the system." Then she saw Addie and her mouth fell open. Alice masterfully hid the shock by bending to kiss Addie's battered face.

Ornella, the nurse, was compact and steady, exuding the reassurance of Florence Nightingale on the battlefield. "It's okay now," she whispered, patting my arm. "Your mother will be fine."

"Don't leave!" Mom cried as, with Ornella's help, we got her settled into a private room and said our good-byes. But when we turned to go, Mom cried out again. "Please don't leave me here!"

Ornella took Mom's hands. "Miss Addie, you stay with me. I'll be right here. You tell those children of yours to go on and get to bed. They are too tired to stay up this late."

I braced myself for a scene. I'd been with Mom day in and day out. She was used to me, she counted on me, and she needed me. But like magic, Ornella magnetized Mother, who smiled like a movie star. "That will be wonderful," she said, pronouncing it "won-da-full," all Katharine Hepburn again. Ornella's soothing light had outshone me.

I wanted Mom to say, "No way! I can't live without my daughter!"

"Maybe I should stay," I said to William.

"Don't be a dope," he grunted. "That nurse is getting twenty bucks an hour so you can get some sleep. We have a lot to do tomorrow, and you absolutely cannot let Mom get dependent on you." He was very stern, and he was right. As soon as I could, I had to leave my mother and go back to my own family. But the first thing I had to do was crawl into a bed and get some sleep.

Needless to say, William and I got a flat tire, but we ignored it and drove, thumping down the highway all the way to our hotel. When we finally got there, the restaurant had just closed.

I played my first sympathy card.

You only get the sympathy card a few times in life. You get it for a reason and you use it when you need someone to bend the rules for you. People feel guilty about using it, but life gives you that card to help you handle all the other bad cards you just got stuck with.

So I played the sympathy card and told the hotel clerk that I had just flown my half-dead mother home, that the plane had broken and we'd had to do the whole journey twice, that I hadn't slept for weeks and hadn't eaten since yesterday (not counting the stale tuna on rye in the plane). Then I told her about the flat tire. She convinced the chef to stay an extra fifteen minutes and feed us, and the bartender gave us a round on the house.

The Marriott was hosting a hairdressers' convention. Ordinarily this is just the kind of thing I'd find deeply satisfying—but when a glittering man with stiff black hair tried to banter, I couldn't do it.

"You, darling, look like you could use a lift—not a *face*-lift, ha, ha, but maybe a little more color in that hair, bring your eyes out, lighten up that brow line." My new friend leaped up and began running a fork through my hair to show me exactly how much better I could look. I sat dumbly while he gave me a zigzag part.

"Not tonight, pal," William said, joining me at the bar after he called AAA to fix the flat tire.

"*Ooh,* your scalp could use a vitamin wrap," the hairdresser said.

"Go back to L.A. where you came from, dear," William said, not unkindly, patting the man on the back.

The hairdresser backed off, and the bartender placed a grilled chicken and Caesar salad in front of me, but I was too tired to eat.

We'd had a plan. The plan was very short-term: Get Mom to New Jersey and come up with a new plan. Now we had the Walter factor to consider, too. Walter was distraught and stayed up all night drinking and pacing the floor. He couldn't orient himself without Mom—and he couldn't find his car keys, which upset him greatly.

Walter's car, an old tank of a Mercedes, had been in the shop for over a year, recovering from a continuous wake of scratches, dents, and collisions. Every time the car got fixed, he'd hit something new on the way home. The autobody people took to following him out of the parking lot in the tow truck, just in case.

We'd all been terrified of Walter's performance behind the wheel, but had been unable to get him off the road. At long last, during the

Florida trip, Cathy seized the opportunity to steal his keys. Now Walter was obsessed with retrieving them.

Three-by-five notecards, executed in Walter's shaky hand, were taped to the front door, the refrigerator, and the bathroom mirror of his and Mom's house. "REWARD! One set of CAR keys in brown leather case. Please return to Walt Huber. Thank you!"

With unflagging determination, Walter called a locksmith, who couldn't make a car key, and the Mercedes dealership, which would neither make a new key nor replace the ignition lock. He even tried to rent a car from Avis. Fortunately, Cathy had also grabbed his driver's license, so that angle failed as well.

Alzheimer's is demanding, uneven terrain for those who have it and for those who care for them. Walter was lucid enough to call Avis, but unable to remember his car accidents. "I'm a good driver," he said, feeling wrongly accused and persecuted. "I've never had any kind of accident!"

Bright and rather early the next morning, Cathy brought Walter to the hospital to see Mother. The room was short of chairs, so Walter perched himself on the high portable commode that stood in the middle of the room. His suit was newly pressed and his shoes shone. His hair was lacquered to perfection.

"How did *you* get here?" he asked me.

"I was with you in Florida."

"Doesn't ring a bell," he said thoughtfully. Walter didn't know he'd been to Florida any more than he knew he was sitting on a toilet. But he remembered his missing keys.

"Do you have my car keys?" he asked me. I shook my head. "Do you have them?" he asked William.

"No, sir. But I can see you are most distressed."

"Yes, I am," Walter answered, gazing absently about the room. "What are we doing here?"

"Visiting me," Mother said.

Walter, remaining seated, shuffled the commode with his feet to the bedside, where he held Mom's hand. William explained to both of them that Mother would have to go into a nursing home for a while.

Mom cried and Walter began to yell. "She wants to go home! I am taking her home!"

"Miss Addie, now calm down. All will be worked out in time," intoned Ornella. "Calm down, Mr. Huber." Walter really hated being told what to do, and it was even harder for him to take orders from a woman.

"Who is she?" Walter sneered.

"The new slave," Mother said, but she tried to whisper.

Mom didn't want to go to the nursing home. She wanted to go home to her own bed, back to health and power, without her busybody, interfering children. She had no awareness of her diminished capabilities and no sense of her needs. The more we tried to gently persuade her, the more she wanted to get rid of us. "You and William just go on home. Walter can drive me," she said, sounding almost like her former self.

"I can't seem to find my keys," Walter told Mom. "Say, do you have them?"

But at that very moment, rational Mom dissolved. "Oh, don't worry about keys, dearest. We don't need them. We can jump out the window and fly home," she said matter-of-factly.

"What?" said Walter. "You can fly? I never knew."

"So can you, but you have to take your shoes off."

"I wouldn't know about that." To Walter's credit, he was not convinced.

Once again, William, Addie, and I were stuck in hospital time, where the passing of hours is marked by the clattering of meal trays. Day fell upon day as William and I pulled strings and pushed paper until, after a week that seemed like a month, we got Addie into a nursing home.

I'd grown up walking by The Glades, where the sagging branches of weeping beech trees hid the cement wheel-chair ramps from the street view. A receptionist behind a glass panel controlled who got in and who got out. Plastic plants and flowers were in abundance, along with large-print signs that read YOU ARE SPECIAL! Megawatt lights and Norman Rockwell prints emphasized a tangible despair. An old lady with a placid face was parked by the elevator. "You are such a slut," she snarled vehemently, just like a sneeze. Then she regained her bland composure.

"Thank you. And you look terrific today, too," I replied. She brightened and gave me a shy smile. Old heads bent forward on frail necks like tulips. Bony hands grabbed at me.

"Please, kill me now," begged an old man with no teeth.

He was intercepted by the floor supervisor. "Nobody is going to listen to that kind of talk," she said and wheeled him away.

"Some residents ask us all the time," sighed the social worker who handled Mom's admission. She pushed a thick stack of paper toward me. By the time I signed the last form, I'd agreed to cover Mom's debts if she ran out of money, which I naïvely believed impossible. I authorized Black's funeral home to collect her body, which made me feel as though I'd taken out a contract on her. I also signed a waiver agreeing the nursing home was not responsible for Mom's health, protection, or "well-being"—in which case, why was I putting her in there?

Mom needed very different clothes for nursing-home life. Talbot's matching skirt-and-sweater ensembles were not going to make it in the weight room. The only place open was Kmart. I headed for the women's section, where a purple T-shirt with HOT GRANDMA emblazoned on it in orange sequins caught my eye. Leopard-print underpants, mules with flamingo-pink ostrich feathers, and a polyester housedress with Day-Glo flowers leaped out at me.

I could just see Mom staggering through the nursing home in a pink sweatsuit embroidered with teddy bears or in those black velour slacks with DETROIT on the rump—revenge for all those years of pleated skirts and Peter Pan collars. Now I had the power. I could make my mother wear whatever I wanted. The shoe was on the other foot, *my* foot. It was the Devil talking to me, and he was persuasive. "Get the cowboy hat!"

"Can I help you?" a saleslady asked, not a minute too soon. And I was quickly on my way with a collection of sensible outfits that my mother would hate as much as I hated all the "sensible" clothes she ever bought me.

When I got back to her room, Mother was not in bed, but sitting in a chair with strange blue and black wires sticking out of the neck of her nightgown. A klaxon buzzed, barely audible over the TV. "I did it myself!" she declared, looking pleased. She'd climbed over the guard rail, cantilevered herself to the floor, and crawled to the chair. "I am all better. I can go home!"

Unbeknownst to Mom (and to me), she was wired to an alarm that no one heard over the Muzak, the radio, and the TV at the nursing station. I asked for help getting Addie back into bed, and a horde of nursing aides descended on the room, yelling at Mom for getting out of bed, yelling at one another for leaving her unattended. No wonder they'd made me sign all those waivers. To discourage any further attempts at independence, they no longer allowed Mother to close her door. The ambulatory residents wandered in at will, pawing at her and scaring her with their demented conversation.

Clearly, Mom needed protection in this place. I got on the phone and called Ornella, that nice nurse at the hospital, who agreed to be Mom's private duty attendant.

William and I barely knew her, but we both had to leave. So we placed Mom's welfare in Ornella's hands, earnestly counting on her to be our eyes, ears, and loving arms until we returned.

Mother sobbed as I said good-bye, and I felt like a traitor for leaving her in a *home*. William and I agreed to look into setting up home care.

Three weeks and two days had passed when I finally got back to my family, and everyone was mad at me. My husband was mad because he'd been doing double time at home and at work. The kids were mad because they felt neglected and were sick of the babysitter, who no longer did anything but sleep on the couch. Even the dog seemed slightly aloof.

"Time to get up," said my husband, standing by the bed, holding out a mug of coffee. I heard the car door slam as he left for work. I rolled to my feet and into my blue jeans. Outside my window I could see the ocean, where "pancake ice" floated in flat, lacy circles on the tide. A crow on a telephone pole cackled and bobbed as it waited to raid the garbage bags set out on the curb for pickup.

In the bathroom, my daughters were bickering over the curling iron. My son—body of a man, mind of a puppy—still slept in his lair, impossible to rouse. I employed the old peanut-butter trick, smearing a thick dollop on his slightly stubbled cheek. Then I whistled for the dog.

The downside was that later I'd have to wash the sheets.

I urged the girls to hurry on my way back to the kitchen, where I lined up lunch bags and filled them with sandwiches, cookies, and fruit. Finally, books and homework had been located and backpacks loaded, and I drove them to school. I wished I could keep them home with me for the day. But I had too much to do.

I returned to a quiet house. I fed the dog and emptied the dishwasher, just as I'd always done. But I couldn't get into the rhythm. A pile of bills, school permission forms, and report cards confronted me. I'd missed parent-teacher meetings, and a new job offer had come and gone. Jittery and disconnected, I sipped at my coffee, trying to find the place in my life where I'd left off, when the phone rang, making me jump, as it would for the next year and a half.

It was The Glades receptionist calling to let me know that my mother was no longer their client. She'd checked out.

Chapter Two

HOME-CARE HOTEL

The drama of living does not abate with age. If anything, it's more intense, because no one expects it to be that way. After my father died, I assumed my mother would become a nice widow who read lots of books, traveled a little, and aged gently unto death. Mom probably had more adventure in mind, but I can say with conviction that she got a lot more than she bargained for in Walter, and not the kind she'd imagined.

After my father died, my mother's social calendar dried up. Apparently, convention among her friends dictates that widows don't get asked to dinner. The husbands don't want to see their own death looming over the salad bowl; the wives don't want to see their future. "They'd rather not invite the Grim Reaper to the table," Mother said jokingly, but she was hurt. For Mother and her friends, status and identity came from a man. Without one, Mother sat at home alone, night after night, and saw her future as an endless string of hollow days.

Walter had known Mom for years. Although our families weren't friends, we went to the same church, the same schools, and of course the same golf club. When Walter's wife died, he called my mother and asked for help with the funeral. He was so helpless and undone, Mother obliged. Afterward, he sent her a thank-you note suggesting, rather oddly, given the time frame, that should he remarry, he hoped a woman like Mom would be his Bride. I told her to chalk it up to grief and distress, and ignore it.

Somewhere along the line, Walter asked Mom out, and Cupid loosed his arrow. For women in their late sixties, suitable dates are hard to find. Walter passed the test. He was ambulatory and good-looking, and he liked to dance. Smitten by love, Mother bought new makeup and updated the hairdo she'd worn for the past twenty years. With joy and enthusiasm, she purchased new high heels and party clothes. She even went to the dermatologist and had her liver spots erased.

It's possible that dementia had been picking at Walter for as long as I'd known him. Looking back, you could see the signs were there from the start. He was already pretty old when he surfaced as Mom's boyfriend, and plenty old enough for Alzheimer's.

In the early days of their romance, Mother was trying to avoid speculation and gossip, so Rob and I, then residing in New York City, were enlisted as chaperones. With us young people along, the occasion would look less like an affair. Those dates were awkward. I'd never imagined Mom having a love interest at her age, plus I couldn't quite get over the sensation that she was being disloyal to Dad, even though Dad hadn't expected her to wither away alone.

Once he said to me, "When I'm gone, don't let your mother marry a man younger than she is. I wouldn't want her to look foolish." Well, Walter was certainly old enough, but the foolish part was out of my control.

On our first double date, Rob and I joined Walter and Mom for dinner at the newly opened Box Tree restaurant in midtown Manhattan. It had gotten great reviews and was terrifically expensive. The place was tarted up like a Venetian palazzo, complete with *putti* and a star-laden sky. The furniture was gilded, the flowers abundant and intoxicating. We had a small, square table, with silver candlesticks and a towering arrangement of roses. The leather-bound menu was like a book. Mother was radiant in a black dress with chiffon ruffles at the surprisingly frisky neckline.

"May I offer you a libation?" asked Walter, snapping his fingers at the waiter, a gesture I had seen only in the movies.

Mom couldn't rope Walter into the conversation, try as she might. He concentrated on his gin and tonic and didn't seem particularly interested in getting to know me or Rob. Instead, he made a point of criticizing the waiter: There wasn't enough bread, the service was slow, and the drinks were watery. He kept asking me if my lamb chops were all right, hoping I'd say no so he could send my plate back to the kitchen.

Occasionally Mother prodded him with "Isn't that interesting, Walter?" to which he nodded. Then he yelled at the waiter again, because the ice in his glass had melted. "Good restaurants serve ice in the water. What kind of a place is this?" he demanded. Mother, of course, had selected the restaurant.

After a few more of these double dates, I learned that almost any dining experience provoked Walter, who was quick to churn a small incident into a nasty confrontation with some hapless waiter. I was puzzled and a little afraid of him, but Mother was blind to his faults.

To her great bliss, Walter was a bona fide opera fan. Dad had gone begrudgingly once or twice a year, but Walter genuinely adored it. He was an enthusiastic weeper, and he and Mother sobbed through the *Ring* cycle together. At this point, I was happy for her. She was back on the town guest list, going to parties, giving parties, furiously making plans. She put her energy into managing Walter—making him call his friends for golf, encouraging him to see his daughter, Cathy—all for his own good, of course.

Mother and Walter moved into the next phase of senior dating. They ate dinner together every night, went to church together, shopped for groceries, and spent most of the summer at his house on the Jersey shore. Mother now managed her own house with much less help. Daisy Brown, five years my mother's senior, did the housework and laundry a few days a week. Frances cooked the occasional meal, until she retired.

I was pregnant with my third child when we moved from New York City to Halifax, Nova Scotia. You'd think I'd have felt I was abandoning my mother, but now that she was running around with Walter, I felt she was abandoning *me*. Even so, every summer thereafter I dragged my family across the border in a car full of graham crackers and baby bottles for the annual pilgrimage to visit Grandmother.

On one memorable trip, when the kids were six years old and younger, Walter answered Mom's doorbell, his withered old-man arm propping open the door, his pants bagging at the knees. "Welcome, welcome!" he said, as he shuffled his feet across the carpet. "Are you staying here?" he asked, warily eyeing our suitcases.

Mother and Walter weren't yet married, and technically Walter lived in his own house. But he had "his" chair in the living room, his spot in the kitchen, and his pajamas in the guest-room drawer. I still thought of Walter as the outsider. Even if I'd never lived in this house, I *had* grown up with all the stuff: the Chinese lamps in the front hall, the ebony coffee table, and the red and gold Oriental rugs. They were "mine" when we were still "us": Mom, Dad, my brothers and sisters, the help, the dog, the cat. But now when Mother said "us" she meant herself and Walter. And to Walter, *we* were the outsiders.

Though I tried to accept him for Mother's sake, Walter did not compare well with Dad, who could make an incidental stranger feel like a long-lost friend. Walter was just plain not interested in people. Of course, Mother's love life was none of my business, but the more I got to know Walter, the more disconcerting it was.

Sensing my skepticism, Mother launched a campaign to mold my relationship with Walter into a happy, familial one. The morning after our arrival, she sat in bed with her coffee, *The New York Times* folded neatly across her lap. Her short gray hair was a little flat from sleeping on it and she had never been so thin. For the first time, Mom looked really old to me, but the stubborn set of her jaw countered any impression of frailty.

"I think it would be lovely to have dinner with Walter," she said.

"What a great idea," I said, lying.

"Yes. And Walter's roses are in bloom. He'd love you to see them." She was envisioning a jolly family dinner at Walter's. I was experiencing a deadly, sinking dread.

Walter's old dowager of a Tudor house resembled an antique store, and was far from childproof. He hadn't changed a thing since his wife died. Glass display cases crammed with china, gilt-edged tables covered with tchotchkes, museum-quality rugs—all were potential disaster zones. The kitchen was equally booby-trapped with dangerous appliances and unlocked cabinets loaded with poisons just waiting for curious children like mine. I did not want to go to his house at all.

As was his custom, Walter arrived shortly after breakfast. "What's all this?" he said, surveying the messy breakfast dishes and a child's pink bunny slipper on the kitchen floor. He had totally forgotten we were visiting. Kicking the bunny slipper out of the way, he advanced on the coffeepot, scowling. Mother gave him his special mug, and he grunted discontentedly as he poured himself a cup. To appease him, she quickly cleared the table, clattering the china into the sink as he planted himself in his special chair, the one I'd been sitting in. "Arragh," he growled, shaking the newspaper.

Mom waited until he finished with the sports page before starting in. "Your garden is so beautiful, Walter. I really want Meg to see it. Why don't we all come over for dinner?"

Walter looked at her as though she were speaking Greek. "*What?*"

Mother took a breath, and tried again. "Let's have Meg and the children over to your place for supper. So they can see your flowers."

"My *what*?" he asked, as though flowers were totally inappropriate for polite conversation.

"Your *flowers*."

"Oh," he said. "Arragh." And he went back to the paper.

"Walter doesn't want us to come," I told Mom later, when he'd left the room. "The children irritate him. If we eat here, he can leave when he's had enough."

Mother stood stock-still, her hands at her sides. "He loves your children," she said solemnly. "He talks about them all the time."

This was not true. Walter hated being interrupted, he disliked chaos, he disliked noise, and he disliked small children. When my youngest was an infant, he called her "it." He also did not like to share his Bride, and our visits took my mother's attention away from him. He didn't want to host us for dinner; he wanted us to leave town.

The real story was that Mother had to admire *his* nearby grandchildren on a regular basis. Now she wanted him to have her family over for dinner. "This is a disaster!" my husband hissed behind Mom's back. "Your parents are going to get plastered and fight in front of the kids!" I told him I'd keep trying to get us out of it.

By late afternoon, after Mom had had a full day of exposure to her overactive grandchildren, I figured my chances had improved. My mother often leveraged her agenda by invoking someone else's feelings, and I was not above thwarting Addie with her own tactics.

I cornered her as she stood at the stove, stirring a pot.

"Mom, the kids are worn out and cranky. They'd be so much happier to eat here, so I can pop them into bed when they collapse."

"You don't want to disappoint Walter, darling. He's been looking forward to your visit all day." I knew perfectly well that Walter couldn't care less. But Mother had this event scripted, frame by frame: the family sitting around Walter's table enjoying an intimate evening of gentle laughter, the adorable children saying precocious things, and Walter's eyes shining with gratitude toward her for such a warm, harmonious family experience.

Rigid with stubbornness, Mother tugged off her flowery apron to reveal a chic white cotton pantsuit. Two strands of pearls shone against the wrinkly tan of her neck. She was all ready to go. We weren't going to get out of this one.

"I'm going over now to help Walter set the table," she said. "Don't you be late."

As I was breaking the bad news to Rob, we heard Mother gunning the engine, followed by a terrific bang and a splintering crash. Had lightning hit the house? Rob and I froze. Mother came clomping up the stairs, her face white with anger and humiliation. She'd thrown the car into reverse and rammed it through the unopened garage door.

"I've had a little difficulty. The station wagon is stuck in the driveway. Robert, dear, could you please get it back into the garage? I will take the Buick and meet you at Walter's as planned."

Mom wasn't going to let a little car crash slow her down. The only thing that mattered was sticking to the plan. She ducked into the Buick, stamped on the gas, and peeled out of the driveway. Rob and I were left behind to clean up the wreckage.

When we arrived, Walter's dining room table had been set for four, so clearly the kids weren't welcome. "Walter thought you would feed the children in the kitchen. They can watch the TV," said Mother. A small television on the counter was ranting over a mass murder in a post office. When I changed the channel, Walter objected. "I always have that station," he said. Rob and I left the children sitting zombie-like over bowls of pasta, staring at policemen zipping up body bags. I wanted to scream.

The dining room was a dark, wood-paneled box with one window at the end. Green wall-to-wall muffled the clinking of silverware and contributed to the funeral-parlor atmosphere. By way of conversation, Walter said, "Goddamn bossy women," glowering first at me and then at Mom, who ate methodically, ignoring him. He pushed the pasta around on his plate and had trouble getting it into his mouth, and cutting it into bits didn't work, either. "I can't eat this," he said. "This is not a dinner. Who thought this up?"

A crash crescendoed from the kitchen. "What in hell?" Walter shouted. Rob jumped up and ran to investigate.

"Not to worry," Rob called from the kitchen. "Nothing serious." He didn't return. The children, bored by the evening news, had tried to occupy themselves by building a tower out of Walter's pots and pans.

"Goddamn children," Walter said. "Women—damn stupid, interfering whores."

Before I knew what I was doing, I said, "Mother, I have food poisoning. I'm very sorry, but we have to leave." Not waiting for a reaction, I grabbed Rob and the kids, stormed out the front door, and ran for the car.

Walter scared me, and the way he yelled at Mom made me furious. I didn't yell back, because I didn't want to be rude to my mother's aged boyfriend; I'd let *her* yell at him first. But good manners weren't going to help here, because my indomitable mom didn't know how to stand up to a bully like Walter. Dad had never raised his voice to her. My parents didn't argue; they discussed.

"I'm sorry, but we had to go," I told her in the morning.

"Of course you did," she said. "Walter was not very good company." But she didn't say more.

In the end, Mother and Walter got married. At the beginning, Mom had a sensible plan. She would move the two of them into a retirement village. But Walter was worried about appearances. It wouldn't look good to cohabitate without a marriage license, so he proposed with a gigantic diamond ring, which Mom accepted. Then Walter threw a fit and said he didn't want to live with a bunch of old nincompoops and be bossed around by an overbearing staff. Mom's sensible plan was called off, and I thought the engagement should have been called off, too. But Walter threatened to dump Mom if she didn't marry him anyway.

Cathy tells this story the other way around—namely, that Mom was chasing Walter—and I have no idea which version is accurate. Some of us suspected Walter was after Mom's money, though he appeared to have plenty of his own.

Right about the time Mother accepted Walter's proposal and his diamond ring, her ophthalmologist diagnosed her with macular degeneration. She was afraid of going blind and being relegated to an institution. No more opera, no more high heels, no more martinis, no more life. So, after about ten years of dating, marrying Walter seemed like a rational solution. After all, there was nothing wrong with Walter's eyesight.

Mom didn't invite me or any of her other children to this event. "Really, it's just a formality," she said, as though they were filling out a few forms. But I discovered they were married in a church, that Mom bought a special dress and carried flowers. She threw a wedding reception at her house for fifty guests—including Cathy. Why were we excluded? Cathy took pictures, but Mother never showed them to anyone—years later, I found a small album stashed in a drawer. Was she afraid that, if invited, we'd compromise the festivities with obvious, if silent, disapproval? I never really knew. Whenever I tried to probe her, Mom changed the topic, as though desperate to avoid disclosing an embarrassing and humiliating event. (A decade later, Cathy told me how hurt she'd been by this boycott, unaware that Addie's machinations had kept us away.)

Walter sold his cavernous house to Cathy and moved into Addie's modest three-bedroom ranch, originally procured after my father died for the downsized life of a widow. The front door opened directly onto a living room crammed with Mom's bulky furniture, along with a baby grand piano that no one could play and a stereo system than no one could operate.

Under the misapprehension that dim lighting camouflaged her wrinkles, Mom used nothing brighter than a forty-watt bulb. If you wanted a little extra light, just in case you needed to see something, you couldn't turn any lamps on because they were rigged to elaborate timers that no one knew how to reset or dismantle. During the late afternoons in winter, Mom and Walter sat in the dark, waiting for those lights to come on.

I don't have to tell you that when you are used to having your own way, a new roommate is a shock. The old people drove each other crazy. Abruptly, every conversation became a quarrel that deteriorated into name-calling. Mom became just as impossible as Walter, and she didn't have Alzheimer's as an excuse. She even provoked him.

"Remember the time we went to Cape Cod?" Mom says innocently.

"No, I don't recall," replies Walter.

But Mom doesn't back off. "You remember! We went last year."

Walter, trying to fake it: "I don't keep track of these things. They're just routine."

Mom, keeping up the pressure: "We flew to Boston to visit the Cowards and rented a car. Remember?"

Walter, cornered, boils over. "Why the hell would I think about such things?"

Mom comes in for the kill. "And you drove the wrong way on the turnpike and we ended up in New Hampshire!"

Walter, red-faced and roaring: "I don't bother with New Hampshire!"

One year into their marriage, Daisy, who'd been working for Mom long before Walter showed up, called me, which she almost never did. "Mr. and Mrs. H. do enjoy their drinks. They're so relaxed, your mother wears her dressing gown all day," she said. "You better come for a visit."

I'd grown up in a house full of servants. Over the years, longtime employees had retired or died, and when no replacements appeared I didn't think twice about it. Daisy was the only person who knew what went on between Mom and Walter. She saw the growing pile of bottles in the recycling bin, the dented cars, and the bruises, but we did not.

After Walter and Addie married, my brothers and sisters and I were rarely invited for more than a one-day visit, and then, for just one meal. Addie and Walter did a great job of acting almost normal for the span of an afternoon or an evening. If the odd situation or non sequitur popped up, it didn't raise the alarm. After all, there they were, just like always, if a bit *older,* Addie in her familiar skirt-and-sweater set, Walter in his suit and tie, drinks before the meal and good-byes after the dessert and coffee. We had no way of knowing that Mom's sweaters were often stained, and the Band-Aids on her arms and legs were always there. We just didn't know.

So, at Daisy's behest, I got on a plane and arrived, without the kids, in the late afternoon. Mom gave a little shriek of welcome from the kitchen. Even when she was the cook, Mom still made a ritual of changing for dinner. But today her blouse was dirty. "I think it's time for a cocktail," she said, digging ice cubes out of the bucket. I accepted a gin and tonic, as she poured herself a colossal vodka on the rocks and coaxed Walter to turn off the TV. He, too, was dressed for the occasion in a navy-blue blazer, pleated trousers, and a sweater-vest sprinkled with crumbs. The house, which had always been as clean and well organized as a hotel, was neglected, with stains on the carpet and a lived-in odor.

Walter often confused me with my sister, Sophie, from Los Angeles, so he cleverly asked, "Where did you come from?"

"I flew in from Nova Scotia."

"Really? All the way up there?"

"Yes, sir," I said. He ambled off to get his own bucket-size drink.

We sat on the couch in an awkward row, with me in the middle. Mom interrogated me about the plane ride, the kids, the dog, my job, the garden, and my husband. Walter, who had been contentedly staring into space, tapped his watch. "This says three minutes after six," he said. "This means dinner is late."

Mom jumped up and rushed toward the kitchen. I wanted to help, but she insisted I remain seated with Walter, who turned the television back on. Pots and pans clanked and the kitchen fan roared. Finally dinner was served, a disturbing concoction of burned chicken and raw frozen corn. The beverage was vodka. I managed to involve Walter in a lengthy chat about the weather, the one topic he could confidently keep up with.

When the ghastly food had been eaten, Mother and Walter lurched toward the television set. *Wheel of Fortune* boomed at maximum volume. The two of them fell asleep, open-mouthed and snoring, while I cleared the table and scrubbed at a burned pan.

Waking from this impromptu nap, Mom called, "We're coming to help."

She staggered into the kitchen with Walter in tow, the two of them blinking and dazed. I was loading plates into the dishwasher when Walter snarled, "Goddamn you, and get away from there. You're doing that all wrong. That's my job!"

I smiled. He had "goddamned" me so many times I was used to it. "No problem," I said mildly.

"Walter, she's just being polite and helping you," Mother said to shush him, which had the opposite effect.

"What the hell? Shut your goddamn mouth!" he shouted. Then, pivoting and shaking his fist at her, he growled and lunged. Mother shrieked, shielding her head with her arm. I jumped between them. Walter stopped just short of smacking me. Abruptly his legs gave out and, miraculously, he fell into a chair. Breathing hard through his mouth, he looked around, bewildered. I got him a glass of water, which he accepted with a shaking hand. He drank a little and cleared his throat.

"Where am I?" he asked, blank-faced.

"You are sitting in the kitchen." I told him.

"I am?" He wasn't catching on.

"Walter, do you know where you are?" I asked.

He said nothing, stupefied. Mother was frozen in place.

"Walter, tell me where you are." He didn't reply.

"I'm calling the hospital," I said, reaching for the phone.

"No!" Mother yelled. Suddenly in motion, she hurried through a puddle on the kitchen floor and tugged Walter by the arm. "Walter, get up," she said desperately, yanking at him until he stood. "We'll go to bed and all will be fine by morning."

As Mom hobbled away, dragging him by the hand, I noticed a dark stain on the seat of her skirt. Walter paused. "Good night!" he said, with a little wave.

The puddle on the floor at my mother's feet proved to be urine. That night, I did not sleep. As I lay in the guest-room bed, I kept seeing my mother with Walter in tow, the back of her skirt soaked through. Of all the evening's alarming elements, this one made me cry. When the sun rose high enough to call it "morning," I pulled on my running clothes, eased out of the front door, and escaped.

Oldhill is beautiful in spring. Wide streets lined with maples, chestnuts, and magnolias give way to broad lawns and old homes, and these houses, like the trees, stand large and impressive. My mother was born in this town and though she loved to travel, she never wanted to live anywhere else, because Oldhill was "home." Everybody knew her. But over the years, as her friends moved away or died, Mom became some old lady a handful of people remembered, and the town was no longer hers.

I ran past the schools, through the fading downtown, to the house I'd grown up in. The house next door no longer displayed the cast-iron Negro jockeys that my brothers once gleefully painted white in the middle of the night. (The neighbors repainted them black.) Whoever bought the place bulldozed the flower beds, installed a swimming pool, and got rid of the jockeys.

Our house was the same as ever, with yellow paint and black shutters, except Addie would never have hung a fake flower wreath on the front door. Behind that door, for all I knew, my childhood world might still be there: the dark, heavy furniture, the vases of flowers, the dinner gong in the front hall that my brothers made out of a cake pan to poke fun at Mother's pretensions. She laughed, but then she actually used it for years, forgetting it had ever been a joke.

I stared at the house until a teenage girl leaned out of *my* former window and called, "Hey, who are you?"

"*I* used to live here!"

We looked at each other for a minute, and then she waved and I started running. Though impossible to resist, looking back like that is asking for it, because there is nothing you can do but walk away from the sweetness and longing.

I was sitting on Mom's guest-room floor unlacing my sneakers when she teetered in, her flip-flops slapping unevenly. She was in her bathrobe and full of artificial cheer. We chatted for a moment about how we'd both slept and then she said, "I thought dinner was very nice last night." She plopped down on the bed.

Mother didn't believe this for a minute. This was her test balloon, to see exactly what I remembered, and how my version of events compared with hers. We'd had little chats like this before. I sighed and pulled off my sneaker, looking up into her old white face. I was tempted to play along and pretend that her life was normal, but I no longer could. She offered me a shaky smile.

"Mom, do you remember Walter taking a swing at you?"

Her smile faded.

I sat down next to her. "And he blanked out and forgot where he was? I wanted to call the hospital, but you went to bed?"

"No," she said, and she covered her face with her hands.

"He seemed like he was going to hit you."

"Not really," she said. What did that mean? I patted her arm for a few minutes. My proud, bossy mother, no matter how savage and galling, was a known entity. This mixed-up, bewildered, doddery Mom was new. During my sleepless night and morning run, I'd had plenty of time to think about what needed to be said. I could hardly back down now, but I was afraid of hurting her. Clearly, Mom was terribly unhappy, fragile, upset, and afraid.

"Walter scared me to death, Mom. You can't live like this." She peeped out at me. "You need some help or you'll get hurt." I expected her to pull away, but she listened passively. "You don't have to do this alone. We can figure it out together."

She leaned against me, a big bony bird in my arms. A breeze puffed the sheer curtains into a gentle curve at the window. Somewhere down the block, a lawn mower guttered and then roared.

"I already have a plan," Mom said, straightening out of my embrace and tucking her chin down with familiar determination. "I have a plan to take care of everything. And you will be surprised and pleased."

Well. I dared to feel a faint ray of hope. Maybe she knew what she was doing; maybe she had figured out a way to get Walter to move into that retirement place after all, or to ask that nice niece of Daisy's to move in like we'd discussed before. Or maybe, after last night, she was willing to divorce him.

"My plan," Mother announced to me, "is that Walter will have a stroke."

Everybody thinks such things, but few would say so. "That is not a plan, Mother."

"Well, I think it is," she said.

"What if you get a stroke instead?"

She hopped stiffly off the bed and tightened the belt on her bathrobe. "I think it will work my way," she said, and she flip-flopped away.

The Age of Reason was over. I imagined Mom leaving the stove on, burning down the house with the two of them in it, or Walter driving drunk, killing himself, Mother, and innocent others. Or hurting Mom in an outburst of temper.

I tried to intervene, but Walter passed his driver's exam, and Mom was competent, according to her beloved doctor. Even though Dr. Gage failed to return her phone calls and often canceled appointments, my mother refused to say a word against him, and I know his meager attentions were enough to perk Mom up for days.

Surely, Dr. Gage would agree that Mom was no longer capable in the judgment department. I called his office for days, and finally got an appointment for myself. When I met him, I understood. Fortyish, tall, olive-skinned, handsome, and sardonic, Dr. Gage was deeply smart, with shark-like charm. No false humor, no cheeriness. Just wry and dry. When my mother had her gall bladder out, she asked him if she could still drink martinis. "Go easy on the vermouth," he told her.

But I was thrown off when the nurse steered me past his office and into an exam room so cold you could have made ice cubes. I perched on the edge of a table, the paper crackling beneath me every time I shifted, futilely trying to keep warm. After an hour or two, the good doctor stepped through the door, without knocking. He glided onto a stool in front of me, his long legs folding like an umbrella. Even crouching on a stool in his white lab coat, he looked like a matador.

"So?" he said, his way of thawing me out.

"Mom is counting on Walter to have a stroke, and then her problems will be solved."

"I'm sure my wife has similar ideas." His voice was so flat, I didn't know if he was kidding.

"Do you think my mother is incompetent?"

Dr. Gage shifted on his seat, uncrossing his legs and resting his arms on his knees. He looked utterly bored.

"Oh, right, *competence,*" he said. "Like anyone is ever competent."

This was not what I had expected.

"Based on her behavior, do you really think Mom can make sound decisions at this point?" I sputtered.

"People make lousy decisions all the time about who they marry, about what they do with their money. But we don't take away their right to make these stupid choices. Your mother knows who she is, she knows right from wrong, and she can make her desires known. That's good enough for me."

"But she can't make a rational plan!"

"So, who can?" he said, and stood up and left.

Shivering and miserable on that ghastly table, I hated to admit he had a point, but it didn't do me much good.

So I called the obvious authorities, hoping for help. But the lawyer, the police, and the social worker all said there was nothing they could do. "There's nothing you can do, either," the social worker told me. "Something bad will happen, an accident or an illness, compelling them to accept help. We call it the 'precipitating incident.' But until then, you wait." And so I waited, watching the blind lady ride her unicycle as I gasped at her every lurch and wobble.

For another three years, Mom and Walter lived on their own. Worried about them, I contrived excuses to visit, and each time was frightened by their accelerating decline, but I could do nothing about it. Mom fell, and came up with more bruises, but no fractures. Walter dented his car more often, but didn't hit any people. And then, finally, Mom fell down on that street in West Palm Beach.

As badly as I felt about it, I had deposited Mother at The Glades nursing home with relief. Ornella provided any extra care the nursing home staff could not, keeping Mom company from morning till night. At last Mom was being cared for, not to mention controlled, by professionals. My life could return to normal. No more nail-biting, no more full-blown anxiety every time the phone rang. Of course, I was sad that my mother had declined to the point where she couldn't manage, but at least, within these confines, a measure of dignity might be returned to her.

When Mom checked herself out of The Glades, my brief moment

of normal was clearly over. I'd blissfully imagined her stuck in that nursing home for at least a month, as the doctor had said. But Mom was competent until declared otherwise, and she had every legal right to run her own show.

According to all accounts, Walter had shown up at The Glades with an empty suitcase—of course, after Ornella had gone home for the night. Frantically stuffing a random assortment of Mother's belongings into the bag, he pleaded with strangers to give them a ride home. "Please, please, help me and my wife! We want to go home! Help!" he beseeched the orderlies and nurses. Walter can be incredibly convincing when he wants something. "We've been kidnapped! Help us!" he shrieked at the visiting relatives of other residents. "We are prisoners here! They won't let us leave!" Finally the nursing-home administrator ordered a cab to get rid of the agitators.

No one could explain how Walter managed to elude his professional home-care provider, obtain a taxi, and arrive at The Glades with an empty suitcase, not to mention keep the goal of retrieving his Bride stuck firmly in his mind. Someone had planted the idea in Walter's head, and then made all the arrangements, including coping with Mom once she arrived back at home. But at the time, I couldn't come up with a suspect. It certainly wasn't Cathy—the last thing she wanted was complications.

On the fly, Cathy had gone to an agency and hired a Ghanaian man named Edward to look after Walter while Mom was stuck in Florida. I had hired Ornella as emergency protection for our helpless mother in the nursing home. But now Ornella was heading up Mom's home-care team and she found herself stuck with Edward, who was living in the house.

The Departure Lounge, as we all came to call Walter and Addie's residence, spontaneously sprang into being—utterly unplanned.

Thus it happened that my children had barely unwrapped their consolation prizes from Florida when I had to leave them again.

"We have Miss Addie all happy now!" said Ornella brightly when I arrived. Looking very professional in a sharp new nurse's uniform, she added, "And this is Mr. Edward," introducing me to a stout man in a tie and jacket. Mom and Walter were encamped in Mother's room. Propped up in the big double bed, Mom looked tiny. Walter was sprawled in an armchair next to her. The TV, resting precariously on a footstool, had been lugged in from the guest room, the cord twisting into a dangerous noose across the floor.

"Oh, hello, dear," said Mom, as though I'd stopped by on my way home from work. She smiled and held out her hand. I had to climb over Walter to take it, but he didn't seem to mind. In fact, he patted at me kindly, as though I were a familiar pet. "We are looking at those cute things," she said. Mom's eyesight was so bad, I don't think she could really see the TV, which was showing clips of frolicking kittens. "Aren't we, Walter?"

"I don't know anything about it," Walter said, his eyes riveted to the screen.

"Come and sit down," Mom said, patting the bed next to her.

They were both fairly drunk. I mentioned this to Ornella, who angrily shook her head. "He gets them for her," she said, indicating Walter.

I quickly realized I had a lot of problems. Clearly, Mother was not returning to the nursing home, and both parents were back in the cocktail loop. On top of that, Ornella and Edward did not get along.

It was conflict from the start. Ornella took one look at Edward and wrinkled her nose in contempt. Edward took one look at Ornella and licked his lips. What started as mild bantering quickly escalated. Ornella is a first-strike person. If Edward said, "Have you seen my pen?" Ornella was sure to answer, "You telling me I took it?"

"In my country, my father was a king," he declared. That might have been true, but Edward was no prince. He rarely washed his clothes or did his own dishes. The guest room, now his room, smelled like a lair. And Edward believed very firmly that the role of woman was to serve man, namely him.

"Be nice, girl, clean these for me," Edward said, holding out a bag of dirty clothes to an outraged Ornella.

Ornella did not for one minute buy into Edward's "it's a man's world" routine. She was from Camden, New Jersey, where, rumor has it, much of the male population is doing time, leaving all the work and none of the glory to the women. These two were natural-born enemies. According to Daisy, they skirmished from dawn to dusk.

Edward planted himself on a chair in the middle of the kitchen, his hands on his knees in a royal pose. "Be a nice girl, make this man some eggs," he said to Ornella, who'd been up all night with Mom, who refused to wear a diaper and got up every hour on the hour to pee. Edward's eyes were glued to Ornella's bottom, as she rushed around trying to get last night's soiled sheets into the washer and make Mom's breakfast at the same time.

"You looking fine today," Edward said lewdly.

"Don't look at me. Look after your work!" Ornella told him. "You paid to cook him eggs, so cook him eggs."

"Don't tell me what to do!" Edward snapped.

Edward asked me for money constantly. "I help your mother when I don't have to. I hold her chair. C'mon, just a hundred dollars." I brushed him off. Edward didn't work for me. He worked for Cathy. Edward, of course, complained to Cathy that Ornella ordered him around, asked him to do work that was not his to do, and interfered with Walter. Walter, meanwhile, complained that he had no money. Someone in the house was relieving him of his cash on a regular basis.

According to Daisy, Walter frequently interfered with Ornella. He didn't like Ornella taking over his role as Mom's helper, a job he'd been doing, in his mind, for many years. "I don't trust them to do it right," he said, explaining how he helped Mother from her bed to the chair, or from the house to the car. Mother could not walk unassisted because she collapsed onto the floor with no warning. "I can hold her with my strong arm." He held out his arm for me to admire. But Walter was often alarmed and confused, putting Mom at risk with his ministrations.

When Ornella tried to help Mom to stand, Walter got involved. "Goddamn it!" he'd yell at her, while trying to pull Mom toward him, away from Ornella. Then Mom screamed at Walter, "You're hurting me! Stop! Stop!" And then Ornella, forced to act, yelled at Walter, "Take your hands off her, Mr. Huber!"

"You can't tell me not to touch my wife," Walter bellowed, with Mom swaying between them.

Edward refused to intercede. He'd much rather have Walter blow up at Ornella than blow up at him. So Edward just stood there and watched. But complaining about Edward wasn't a good way to promote the peace between me and Cathy, who often said, rather broadly, "Edward loves my father. They get along great." Very few men are professional caregivers. Cathy had been lucky to find Edward at all, and Walter really did require help from a man.

Since both parents needed attending around the clock, no one could leave the house to get groceries. This was less of a problem than you'd think, because neither Ornella nor Edward could cook. They fed our parents a steady diet of cold cereal, canned soup, and frozen dinners, all in front of the TV. Save for a couple of cartons of milk and juice, the refrigerator was empty.

Nor could Edward drive. This meant that if Walter had an appointment, Cathy (who had a baby and a toddler at home) had to take him. Everyone knew Ornella could drive, but she didn't feel that driving Walter was her job. Furthermore, if Ornella left the house, Edward would be in charge of Mom, and he was not about to take her to the bathroom—not that Mom would have let him.

Edward lived in five days a week. Then Agatha, a tiny African lady, took over responsibility for Walter on the weekend. Ornella was supposed to work seven days a week, with her best friend, Astrid, taking the night shift. But even though she needed the money, Ornella conceded she didn't have the stamina to work all seven days, and Astrid couldn't work all seven nights, either. So Ornella arranged for several of her friends to cover the weekends. In addition, remnants of Mom's old regime—Daisy, Luanne, and Max—brought the gilded memory of a past when Mom was queen into the present. When Daisy and Max were in the house, Mother brightened. Max was a deaf, beat-up, sweet old man who did hardly anything but push a broom or rake a few leaves. Luanne helped Mother sort out her bills.

Daisy, Luanne's mother, older than my mother, laundered Mom's clothes and dusted. I thanked God they were there, because I got crucial surveillance from them.

Eleven people were now on the payroll, and no one on site was in charge. Our growing staff was cramped in Mom's three-bedroom house. They got on one another's nerves, bickering nonstop.

Try though you may to concoct a fail-safe care plan, it's impossible to get it right, because the minute you come up with a strategy, the situation changes. Fresh, nasty developments force you into stopgap contingencies that then become the status quo. Who can come up with a rational, well-thought-out plan when the night shift isn't covered?

Simplicity is the key to running a show like this, but William and I had not yet grasped that principle. We were plugging holes in the dyke with people who were late for their shifts or didn't show up, and people who didn't get along. More and more people went in and out of the house, walking into my mother's bedroom, leaving her without privacy or refuge, and taking her stuff. But, at first, because nothing of value went missing, it didn't seem worth throwing a wrench into our precariously constructed system. We just kept adding more people to the payroll, solving one problem at a time, because living so far away, that was about all we could manage.

The house itself was not conducive to harmony. Each room was awkward and abrasive, reflecting the emotional state of the inhabitants. You couldn't face a person comfortably without twisting your neck. You couldn't cross a room without hitting your shin on a footstool or bumping a table, a terrible setup for a stroke patient with a head injury who was also going blind. Danger lurked everywhere. Nor was the house set up for an Alzheimer's patient. The kitchen (gas burners, sharp knives), the phone (solicitors and outright thieves), and the mailbox (sweepstakes and once-in-a-lifetime offers) were potential disaster sites, as was the vodka bottle. The exterior doors, of which there were many, could all be opened from the inside, allowing Walter to escape unnoticed.

Alzheimer's patients do best in calm environments, where confusion is minimized. Walter was not getting that kind of support. Except for perhaps Edward, he could not recognize the various care workers. He was constantly bumping into strange women who told him not to touch his own wife, in his own home. As long as I'd known him, Walter had an authority problem with women, especially if he'd had a few drinks. He was currently drinking quite a bit. And he didn't like to drink alone.

"Care for a libation?" Walter asked me at ten o'clock one morning. He stood in the kitchen in his silk paisley bathrobe, his skinny bald legs on display when the fabric parted. When I mentioned the time, he said, "No time like the present," and poured an ounce of tonic into a tall glass, followed by six ounces of vodka.

"Walter, if you drink that, you'll get drunk," I told him.

"I don't think so," he said.

"I think you mixed up the tonic with the vodka."

"That's how you make a vodka tonic," he said. "You mix them up."

"How's about you make another one, and pour the vodka in first?"

"Don't tell me how to make a drink!" he snarled. But he made himself another.

I was right. When he started with the vodka, he mixed the drink properly. "Here, you take this one," he said and waved the triple-strength version at me.

Walter took a big swig. "Here's to your health," he said. I took a tiny sip to placate him.

"Edward, Edward! Your man drinking again!" hissed Ornella into the spare bedroom, where Edward was engrossed in a morning talk show.

Daisy, observing from her ironing board, shook her head. "I'm just glad your father's not here to see this," Daisy said to me loudly.

"Who said the man cannot have a drink?" came Edward's reply.

Tiny Daisy put down her iron and limped over to the breakfast table, where Walter sat with his drink. "Now, Mr. Huber, you haven't had your orange juice yet this morning."

"I haven't?" asked Walter, docile when Daisy was in the house.

"No, sir. But I am going to make you a big glass. Give me that now." Daisy glared and took mine away, too. *"Letting that man who don't know more than a baby get himself involved with a cocktail at ten o'clock in the morning,"* she muttered as she poured Walter his orange juice and poured the vodka tonics down the drain.

William called me from Colorado for a briefing. "How's life at the Departure Lounge?" he asked.

I really didn't know where to start. "Let's just say the drinks are outrageous, and they never run out of nuts."

Even though eleven people were being paid to look after Mom and Walter, no one was being paid to look after the housekeeping. Not counting Daisy, who, at eighty-two, was not exactly the White Tornado. On this visit, and on many that followed, I ran myself ragged, and so did William, when he was there. I cleaned the house, cooked, and froze enough dinners to last two weeks, went grocery shopping, restocked the Depends and the boxes of rubber gloves and Fleet enemas that had become household staples along with flour, sugar, and toothpaste.

I also bought a vacuum cleaner and a microwave. The pharmacy let me open an account, as did the wheelchair-rental people. I met with a bank manager and explained the situation. She had known Mom for years, and agreed to watchdog Mom's account for suspicious or crazy transactions.

I did laundry and picked up dry cleaning. I drove Mom to doctor appointments, scheduled physical therapy, and scheduled more doctor appointments. I bought another television set for the staff and had cable installed. Luanne and I locked up the silver and Mom's jewelry and filed her papers in a secure cabinet. I took the car in for service, had the rugs and upholstery shampooed, and replaced the garbage disposal broken by Agatha's fork.

And after Walter climbed inside the fireplace to light the gas, which had already been on for a while, I got the gas turned off. I don't know why the house didn't explode when he lit that match. He was unhurt and unsinged, but it was a very close call.

I bought and installed four cordless phones to eliminate the phone-cord hazard, relegating the old ones to the trash can. But Mother couldn't come to grips with the new phones and insisted on speaking into the earpiece. The handsets wandered around the house, getting lost. Now, when I called Mom from Nova Scotia, I hardly ever got through.

The whole blasted setup was wrong, a lousy composite, cut-and-pasted together with plenty of potential for disaster. But William and I didn't have the time to put a new plan, with new people, into place. I just hoped that the staff would show up for work, that Mom and Walter wouldn't be too nasty to them or to each other, and that the whole thing would hang together until one of us could return. Once again, I left my helpless mother in the care of total strangers, some of whom I'd never even met.

But I'd been gone for another two weeks. I had to get home.

Chapter Three

MELTDOWN AT THE DEPARTURE LOUNGE

Supervision of the constant and creative variety was crucial at the Departure Lounge to keep all those moving parts moving. Because Addie had always been so commanding, this was a responsibility that none of us—not me, William, Sophie, nor my brother Roland in Canada—had realistically envisioned. Sophie couldn't make the trek from California more than a couple of times a year. Roland's career as a lawyer wouldn't let him off the hook. But as Alice lived close by, she gamely agreed to act as the emergency first responder until someone else could get there to take over.

Every three weeks or so, William or I took a shift at the Departure Lounge to shop, cook, freeze dinners, clean, take care of repairs, talk to doctors, rally the staff, have lunch with Alice for fun and comparing of notes, and cheer up the inmates. Sophie and Roland came when they could. Addie kept saying she'd cover our airfare but, given her wobbly mind, I ran this provision past her lawyer and the bank to ensure she could afford to, and that we weren't taking advantage. I would not have been able to manage otherwise. As it was, my husband resented paying for extra babysitters. I lost my fund-raising job, though I continued to snatch freelance work when I found it. It was exhausting. But I was compelled. I believed there was no alternative because come Judgment Day, I wanted to be recognized as a good daughter.

My family and friends in Canada knew me as a soccer mom in grass-stained blue jeans. I drove an old van full of dog hair and candy wrappers, the front bumper tied on with a bungee cord. And really, I am grateful to the sport, because I now know every back road and dead end in the province. Most of my fellow soccer moms grew up in Nova Scotia and their directions were generally unhelpful to an immigrant like me. "You turn left where Fred's barn was before it burned down" was typical guidance. Responsible for half the girls on my daughter's "twelve and under" soccer team, I maintained contingency supplies: food, magazines, CDs, tampons, bug spray, hair elastics, Band-Aids, duct tape, and chewing gum.

Several days a week, the athletes, smelling like watermelon hair gel, crammed into the van (which those darlings referred to as "The Shitmobile" behind my back). Armed with MapQuest, I struck out, passing meadows brimming with Queen Anne's lace or winding along a shining shoreline, almost happy, praying the cell phone did not ring.

If our journey was long, a slow leak in one tire often forced me to pull over, plug a compressor into the lighter socket, and pump it back up. I once found myself lost in the cul-de-sac of a housing development so new, the street signs weren't up. A cloudburst like Niagara Falls pounded on the van, complete with zigzag lightning, and the girls shrieked and hollered with fear and glee, while I attempted to reinflate the tire without being electrocuted. Drenched, I got myself back in the car, and the cell phone rang. Alice reported, from the emergency room, that Addie had fallen in the bathroom and hit her head. Walter, who had insisted on accompanying her to the hospital, fell off his chair in the waiting room and hit *his* head. (That is, if I understood Alice correctly, with the girls screaming, the thunder and rain pounding in the background.) Mom had been stitched up and released, but Walter, yelling and foaming, had been admitted for observation. Alice, hoping to get back to her office, signed off. The rain stopped, I looked at the map—no help in this nameless place—and hit the gas with nothing but blind faith to guide me.

But I switched to my alternate identity when I landed at Newark Airport: an unmarried American with no children. A professional in a black polyester pantsuit with a bulging briefcase, I lived in a hotel, drove a rental car, and managed a private nursing home. My clients were my parents. I spent much of my time in appointments with doctors, lawyers, and bank people, managing a staff that quickly swelled to fifteen people as we kept adding shifts, and an annual budget that ballooned to $400,000.

Though a thousand miles away, the chaos at my mother's house leaked into mine. The steak on sale at the supermarket was a pretty good deal, which made up for the strawberries at about a dollar each. I grabbed paper towels and toilet paper, crossing them off my list. Depends were on sale at half price. I wrestled the oversize carton onto the shopping cart, feeling pleased with myself. It wasn't until I was jamming the box into the trunk that it dawned on me I was not in Oldhill, New Jersey, but in Halifax, Nova Scotia. My family was enjoying those fleeting years between Huggies and geriatric briefs. They could all make it to the potty on their own. You just don't know enough, at the time, to appreciate it.

In addition to Depends, I became aware of a whole line of products previously invisible to me. There are enemas—which incidentally, you can also purchase by the case; hair-dryer holders (so you can use both hands on your do); and giant bibs to help cut down on dry-cleaning bills. Those urinal bottles might come in handy when you're stuck in rush-hour traffic. And just think how great my legs would look if I started wearing pressure stockings *now.*

I caught myself admiring the peppy colors of those anodized aluminum walkers with their nifty flip seats so you can sit down while you shop. I'm sure shopping the mall with my teenage daughters would be less of an ordeal if I could sit down anytime I wanted.

Aging feet were a revelation to me, with their arthritic toes, ingrown nails, and knobby bunions. Most old people can't cut their own toenails, but they rarely tell you. It's too humiliating an admission. You'll be on close terms with a podiatrist and the good Dr. Scholl, grateful for his moleskin and his corn plasters. And it's never too soon to wear orthopedic shoes if you think about it.

The fabulous Ferragamos and Pappagallos Mom was accustomed to weren't any good for her problem feet. But Addie rejected the comfortable models I proffered. When she went out, Mother crammed her feet into fancy shoes, even if they crushed her toes and made them bleed. And at home she insisted upon beat-up blue suede flats that, worn out long ago, she'd held on to for gardening. I almost got her into a pair of three-hundred-dollar Eccos. Addie took them for a test drive, swaying down the hall and into the living room, where Walter, with laser-beam accuracy, zeroed right in on her feet.

"I call those *clodhoppers,*" he said, shaking his newspaper and turning the page. Needless to say, the Eccos went back into their box.

Sophie tried, too. I was in residence for the UPS arrival of two classy pairs of sandals, one black and one tan, from Talbot's.

"Send them back!" Mother said. "I have no want of these." I don't recall what she didn't like about the shoes. I think it was the idea that we, her daughters, were acting as if we knew best.

I couldn't stay with Mother and Walter, thank God, because Edward was housed in the guest room. Located a few miles from Mom's house, the Devonshire Inn could have been called "Miss Havisham's Bed and Breakfast." It was not for everyone, which is why it always had a vacancy. While you might prefer a room that didn't evoke generations of inhabitants, the Devonshire was a real place, and you were a real person in it.

The Devonshire had been on its last legs for decades. Originally designed as a genteel retirement home back in the 1920s, the three-story building sat back from the street on a horseshoe-shaped drive. Oaks, beeches, and pines threw shade across the capacious front lawn. At a distance, the place looked intact.

A flagstone terrace ran along the front facade, where white wrought-iron chairs and tables were encouragingly arranged. A few stubborn rosebushes insisted on staying alive in the neglected garden. Sighing with longing for bygone days, the door opened onto a front hall crowded with drab arrangements of dried flowers, and glass cases displaying china swans, rhinestone earrings, and homemade soap. These desirables could be purchased at the front desk, if an employee happened to be there.

The atmosphere inside the Devonshire was unparalleled. An indoor fountain surrounded with sphagnum moss and fake flowers trilled in the center of the living room. A white wicker coffee table sat in front of a leather chesterfield, flanked by two velour lounge chairs, across from a Victorian loveseat and Danish modern couch. Strangers in pastel portraits (purchased at garage sales) stared unnervingly out of dusty, ornate frames. William had to look closely to determine that a handsome gray-haired couple wasn't Mom and Walter.

Sure, the sheer funkiness of the Devonshire was creepy—the wear and tear of human life was beyond obvious. But real people from decades past had sat on the ottoman (possibly not yet threadbare), perhaps staring out the window and up into the trees as evening fell, and this lingering presence was oddly comforting. Though nothing lasts, perhaps something familiar and kindly sticks around, at least for a while. The Devonshire embraced the inevitability of decline, the perfect counterpoint to the delirium of resistance at my mother's household.

As Mom's physical condition improved after her fall, life at the Departure Lounge got worse. The stronger she got, the more active she became. And now she got dressed every day, if not exactly the way she used to, turned out in a wardrobe reorchestrated by Ornella. The pink-and-white Chanel jacket, paired with a brown pleated skirt, green kneesocks, and the blue suede shoes springs to mind as particularly unique.

Compared with the careful, dignified dresser she'd been, Mother now looked like a scarecrow. But if the past was your yardstick, all you got was Mom, pathetic and diminished, which didn't do you or her much good. If you tossed out the yardstick, you could see how bravely she tackled her new life—an inspiration even in those singular clothes.

Before her fall and stroke, one of Mother's more trying traits was her bona fide know-it-all stance. She had, after all, read the entire Compton's Encyclopedia and remembered every detail. No matter what topic you opened your mouth on, she knew more about it than you, which had been incredibly annoying. The new Mom shuffled facts with crazy images that made for a whole new kind of conversation.

"Walter is making me cold, cold noodles, and whoosh! Those crows fly away in the best of times."

"You've always liked crows, and noodles, too," I said, pleased with myself for recalling that a caregiver manual advised playing along, no matter what the "confused" person (a.k.a. Mom) said.

"Hugin and Munin," said Mom.

Because of my mother, I happened to know that Hugin and Munin are the two mythical ravens "Thought" and "Memory," who sit on the shoulders of the Norse god Odin, giving him daily world news reports. If the noodles were a reference to her brain, Mom was trying to tell me that Walter was making her brain-dead! Her thought and memory might have flown away—but in a very weird way, Mom was as sharp as ever. You just needed very broad terms of reference to chat with her.

A physical therapist came to the house three times a week, and soon Mom was clomping around with a walker, which she hated and was determined to ignore. With no warning, she'd abruptly stand up, lunge a few wild steps, and collapse onto the floor. The living room was a death trap. The corners of the coffee table, the piano bench, the brass standing lamp—all potential trips to the emergency room. Watching Mother was nerve-racking. You just wanted to tie her to a chair so you could relax for five minutes.

And that was an option. Dotty people in nursing homes get put in "gerry chairs," adult-size versions of those baby seats on wheels, with the tray across the front. Sedation was another option, but I knew Mother would rather careen around the house, risking broken bones and driving the rest of us crazy. There may be a certain dignity to sitting quietly in an armchair all day long, instead of falling on your face, but it doesn't resemble living. At least Mother felt victorious almost as often as she felt defeated. It was the rest of us who needed the tranquilizers.

Meanwhile Walter, continuing to erode mentally, was working overtime. One morning, Mom flapped her wings and fell in the living room. As Ornella helped her up, Walter rushed in and punched at Ornella, yelling, "What have you done to her?" He missed her that time. As the day wore on, Mom got restless and wanted a little action. So she and Ornella ventured forth to make a slice of toast. Walter, imagining Mother was going to get burned, threw Ornella aside and grabbed Mom's arm, bruising her to the bone.

In the afternoon, when the physical therapist lifted Mom's good arm over her head, Walter bounded in out of nowhere, screaming, "You can't do that to my wife!" The therapist quit. That night at 4 A.M., Walter believed the fire alarm was going off and called 911. No one else could hear a fire alarm, but Walter could. The firemen arrived and were not pleased to learn there was no emergency.

Walter started out the following day with his usual round of breakfast gin and tonics. Mother fell. As Ornella lifted her, Walter launched a two-fisted frontal assault. Ornella managed to duck the first punch, but the left hook caught her on the jaw. Edward was nowhere to be found. Ornella called the police, who called me in Halifax. Walter, Edward, and Ornella were shouting at one another in the background, punctuated by Mom yelling, "Stop it!" at the top of her lungs.

"Okay, buddy, calm down," a male voice said, presumably to Walter. "Mrs. Federico? This is very confusing here."

I heard the other officer saying, "No more drinking. I am a policeman, and you are not going to drink anymore!"

"Just find all the booze and pour it out," the man on the phone said to his partner. Meanwhile, Edward and Ornella were still shouting. "Knock it off. Which one of you is in charge?"

"I am!" Ornella and Edward said in unison.

The officer on the phone said to me, "Look, I don't think you want me to arrest your father."

I resisted the impulse to say, *That would be ideal.* "Could you please file a report, Officer?"

"You need to get these people into a home or something. They shouldn't be drinking, and I don't want to get called up here again." Then he hung up. *Of course* neither Walter nor Mom should be drinking, but the staff was afraid to refuse them. Technically, Mom and Walter paid their wages, and no one wanted to get fired.

Drinking had always been an essential and sacred institution in my family. I grew up watching my parents have cocktail hour, rain or shine. Dad got home from the train station at 5:45 every night and proceeded straight to the bar. Before I was born, perhaps those martinis had been made in a shaker, but in my day, Dad filled two glasses up to the brim with gin and skipped the vermouth.

Mom always sat on the loveseat wearing her dinner outfit: white blouse, black skirt, pearls, and pearl earrings. She drank most of her martini in three gulps, tactfully managing to set the glass on the table without completely draining it. Then, with one eye on her lipstick-smudged glass, she waited for the moment when Dad heaved himself out of his chair and said, "Addie, how about a dividend?"

For a moment, Mother pretended she might not have one. But she always said, "Oh, I guess so," her eyes following him the three short steps to the bar. After she'd gotten the glass into her hands and had another big gulp, relief softened her features. It was all right. She'd gotten her second drink, and she might even get a third.

There were drinks at noon, drinks before dinner, and then perhaps nightcaps. You invited people over for drinks; and you met for drinks at bars, in clubs, and before the opera. Mother always kept a bottle of champagne in the refrigerator, just in case life needed celebrating. To give up drink was to disclose a social infirmity, and everyone knew you couldn't trust a man who wouldn't have a drink. It was not surprising that Ornella could hardly keep Mom off the sauce, unless she was willing, and she wasn't, and Walter was happy to offer her a libation.

I often imagined that Mother's life would be better, on the whole, without Walter in the picture. (I knew *mine* would be.) He wasn't all that serene before his dementia kicked in, and Alzheimer's disease hadn't improved his temper. At first, anyway, William and I perceived Cathy as her father's agent, working against our mother's interests to promote his. For one thing, Mother had already set us up to see Cathy in a less than favorable light.

Cathy lived in Oldhill with her husband and two small children. She'd married late in life and was busy running around after little kids. I only ever saw Cathy at my mother's house during the excruciating Christmas luncheons or Easter dinners that Mom put on. Cathy sensibly stuck to the sidelines drinking iced tea, while we ignored her.

Although for years Mother sat at Cathy's table for all the minor holidays and a few of the major ones, Mother painted Cathy as a tedious personage whom she graciously endured out of love for Walter. Furthermore, Addie hinted that Cathy's interest in her father was completely self-centered; she did not have Walter's interests at heart, only her own—namely, money. Not only all that, but as far as Addie was concerned, Cathy was rude, showing Mother insufficient deference, unaware that Mom was a member of a royal family, namely, ours.

Cathy wasn't exactly in love with us, either, because we were not very nice to her. This unfortunate dichotomy undermined the early stages of our mutual home-care plan.

The current setup might barely hold up for Addie, but it was no good for Walter. Too many faces, too much commotion, and a lack of routine jangled his nerves. He blew up a couple of times a day, which made people less than supportive and more impatient with him. "Why don't you replace Ornella with attendants from the agency I use?" Cathy suggested. I snorted with disdain.

William and I shook our heads. From our lofty perspective, poor Cathy couldn't admit her father was a lost cause, a demented liability headed for oblivion. Instead of facing the cold, hard truth and putting him in an institution *tout de suite,* she was blaming our beloved Ornella and company.

We thought this was so outrageous, we took Cathy's bland suggestion as an affront. Our Ornella was a welcome pillar of sanity when we arrived from Florida that dismal night, an understanding, empathetic friend in time of crisis. We were loyal, plus she was on our side. She didn't like Walter, either.

There was also the race card: old, uncomfortable territory for me for many reasons. Ornella and her team were black, and I felt guilty about being white, or rather, about not being black. As a child I was simultaneously yanked toward the black people who *worked* in our home (and looked after me) and toward "us" white people, who *lived* there. Black women cleaned the bathrooms, washed the clothes, cooked my food, and held me tight—all in exchange for a paycheck dispensed by my mother. But as a child, I didn't know that.

Each day of my childhood life began with a black woman. Every morning at six o'clock, I watched from my window as a taxi pulled into our driveway and Millie Smith climbed out. I heard Millie muttering as she clomped up the back steps, fishing the keys out of her capacious purse, and opening the kitchen door.

Millie Smith was short and very old. Her mother had been born in slavery. Of course, I learned that fact from my mother, not from Millie. Millie worked for us, and Millie's sister, Mary, worked for my aunt across town. I'm sure they had a lot of stories to swap.

Millie had a deep bass voice that got deeper when she was mad and huge hands with long, fantastic nails that were hard as iron. She told me it was from dipping her hands in laundry starch. Millie believed that her good health was due to her diet: menthol cigarettes and vanilla ice cream. Once in a while, I saw her eat a piece of white toast.

Each morning, Millie went down to the basement to hang up the woolly coat that had been my sister's and change into her uniform, a striped dress covered with a white apron. She sat on the painted yellow chair at the foot of the steps, tying the white leather shoes with crepe soles that she wore at work, along with "flesh"-colored stockings—white-people flesh. Her legs didn't match the rest of her when she had them on.

I spied on Millie as she carried the coffee tray up the front steps to my parents' bedroom door. Coffee almost always spilled into the saucers, eliciting Millie's exasperated sigh. She'd lower herself down to her knees with difficulty, so she could use both hands to dump the coffee back into the two cups, wiping the saucers clean with her apron. Then she'd heave herself to her feet, leaving the tray on the doorstep.

"Miz Hen? Time to get up." (Though our family name was Henry, she always referred to either of my parents as "Miz Hen.")

I watched as she'd tighten her hand into a fist and rap on their door, hard.

"Coffee get cold," she called before turning on her heel and heading downstairs to open the curtains, readying the house for the day.

There were more people working in our house than living there. Millie did the laundry; Gladys, Didie, and later Emma did the cooking. Myrtle and then Frances did light housework and minded the children. Charlie, then Thomas, did yard work. Winston was briefly Dad's chauffeur.

One morning, Millie's brother-in-law drove her to work. Her little nephew, about my age, held on to her neck and wouldn't let her out of the car. That was my Millie he was hugging. Millie giggled, something I had never heard, and she covered him with kisses, something she'd never done to me.

I'd assumed I was family to Millie. But after that morning, I began to understand that I was not, that she didn't think of me as belonging to her that way. Millie, Frances, and all those others who came to our house, who took care of me and held me when I cried, did so because I was their *job*. All through the years I'd loved them, looked up to them, and depended on them—it made me hate myself. I wasn't theirs.

When I turned six, I wasn't allowed to eat a cozy dinner in the kitchen with the help anymore. Abruptly, I found myself on the *other* side of the swinging door, seated with my family, and my former dining companions had to serve me. You were forbidden to strike up a conversation with Frances as she proffered the potatoes in a silver dish. You could whisper a thank-you, but otherwise you had to pretend she wasn't there.

Now *I* was the white boss lady in a very similar and disturbing setup. *I* was in charge, paying people to be "like family" to batty Mom and cranky Walter. Ornella, for her part, had to put up with two crazy and unpleasant old white people because I couldn't do it myself. And Cathy suggested we dump Ornella to improve life for the evil Walter? I hardly bothered to answer her. Besides, we didn't want a house full of employees like Edward.

Edward did almost nothing but wake Walter up in the morning and put a box of cold cereal on the kitchen table next to an empty bowl and a spoon. Walter even shuffled to the fridge for his own milk. Edward continued to hit on me for money. But when Cathy showed up, he was as busy as a bee, holding her chair, asking how her children were. He practically skipped around the room holding hands with Walter to demonstrate their great relationship.

William and I insisted on keeping Ornella, and things got worse. Ornella slapped Edward with a sexual harassment suit for constantly grabbing her behind. The day after the police came, she showed up to work with "the Reverend," her church pastor, for protection against Edward and Walter. The Reverend sat on a chair in the front hall and didn't move. But, at Ornella's request, he went on the payroll.

"He her boyfriend!" Edward told me.

"No he not!" hissed Ornella.

Mom kept getting stronger, but her mental state never stabilized. One day, she was almost her old self. The next day she was talking to the man on the ceiling again. And as she got better, she also got bored.

Ornella often answered the front door to find a deliveryman with a TV set and a case of scotch. Mom couldn't see well enough to dial the phone, but Walter could. Together, they called liquor stores and placed large orders. The stores were only too happy to oblige and took credit cards over the phone. There were fifty liquor stores in a twenty-mile radius. I called as many as I could and asked them not to take Walter's orders. But I couldn't get them all. If it wasn't booze, it was TV sets. Walter was having trouble working the remote, so he thought the set was broken. And unfortunately, he couldn't remember that he'd already placed an order, so more TV sets kept showing up. That made him very angry. "Who thinks they can send us these things?" he said.

The UPS man and the FedEx lady became regulars at the house. "There's two more TVs. What you want me to do with them?" Ornella asked me, a million miles away in Canada. I added "Return Unusual Purchases" to my list.

Mom, presumably tiring of frozen entrees, hired a cook herself, also over the phone. Cassandra Paris showed up like the Second Coming, and took over. Unlike most of the people who worked for my parents, Cassandra did not dress to please the old white folks. She showed up in T-shirts and jeans, or vivid party dresses, outrageous braided and sprayed hairdos, and fabulous nails. Cassandra rapidly became the household manager. Competent and combative, she was Guyanese, and considered herself superior to any staff from the Caribbean, Africa, or the United States.

Cassandra bossed everyone around until fights broke out. She forced me to become a fast-talking diplomat, smoothing over relations with heart-to-heart talks behind her back, often long-distance. She was educated, confident, and efficient, and the only staff she didn't look down on was Daisy and Luanne, whom she adored. Ornella and Edward were finally united in common cause: They both hated Cassandra.

But Addie loved her. Now Mom and Walter were enjoying—if not haute cuisine—good, home-cooked food. But as Addie had hired Cassandra herself, a third front in the household conflict was born.

My phone rang off the hook. Someone who was either very angry or completely hysterical was sure to be on the other end, full of upset, indignation, resentment, blame, or legal problems. My other family life spiraled into a chaotic mess because I couldn't pay attention, distracted by worry and constant calls from New Jersey. I burned so many dinners that I started to photograph the more stunning results: asparagus like sticks of charcoal, a cartoon steak charred black and crispy, and a chicken in a melted plastic bag, because I'd jammed it into the oven without unwrapping it.

Round circles embellished the outside deck, where I had frantically deposited burning pots and pans, trying to head off the smoke alarm, because if it went off, I had to drag out a ladder, rip off the cover, and yank out the battery, leaving something else to boil over in the process. Finally, so I could talk on the phone no matter what else I was doing, I got a hands-free headset. But some problems had to be handled in person.

"I can't work with Astrid," said Ornella. "She's late, she's lazy, and she doesn't respect me. I think she's putting some kind of spell on me, because I've been waking up with terrible pains in my legs."

Since the beginning—which seemed like ages ago, but had been a couple of months, according to the calendar—Astrid had taken the night shift with Mother. Tall, slender, and quiet, Astrid came with a letter of reference from her previous employer, something most people in our employ didn't have.

"But, Ornella, she's your best friend!" I said. "That's why we hired her."

"Astrid has turned against me," Ornella said solemnly.

Mom's inclination to create a bit of drama to amuse herself was not harmless. It turned out she'd fueled this conflict by playing Astrid and Ornella off each other, listing the defects of each to the other as though in complete confidence. It's the way she raised us children and managed most family relations.

Ornella called again. "Astrid is putting voodoo on at night, in your mother's bedroom. I'm finding bones and feathers under the bed."

This is not the kind of thing you expect. It was too exotic, too ridiculous for Ornella to invent. I also knew a tiny bit about voodoo—namely, that it isn't the black zombie magic popularized in old Hollywood movies. "This is very disturbing for a Christian woman like your mother," Ornella said, bolstering her position. I frankly doubted that Mom was disturbed by a few bones. All those volumes of the encyclopedia had made her curious and open-minded. "Well, it's very disturbing for a good Christian woman like me," Ornella countered.

I called Astrid.

"I say a few prayers," she admitted.

"What about the chicken bones?"

Astrid laughed. "She says that? There are no bones."

Bones or no bones, I wasn't going to fire anyone for her religious beliefs.

Then Ornella called to report that Astrid was physically abusing Mother. "Her arms are bruised this morning. And last night, those bruises weren't there." Mom did have an awful lot of bruises, but how had she gotten them during the night, other than from falling in the bathroom? I asked Mom if she was afraid of Astrid.

Mom, having one of her slippery-dippery days, replied, "A black thing comes," which was inconclusive at best.

Of course Astrid denied it. But I couldn't believe Ornella would go to all this trouble to get rid of her without good reason. I could neither prove nor disprove the abuse accusation. It was Astrid's word against Ornella's, and Ornella was in charge. It was all pretty fishy, but even though we were pretty sure Ornella was lying, William and I didn't have much choice but to fire Astrid.

I had never fired anyone in my life. The next time I visited, I took Astrid aside and handed her a box of Kleenex. "Astrid, I am letting you go," I said, forcing myself to look her in the eye like a real boss lady. She started wailing and kept it up for an hour, until I started crying, too. Finally I wrote her a whopping severance check, and she stopped crying, got in her car, and drove away.

I escaped to the Devonshire Inn. The doorknob to my room came off in my hand but the owner, who was not the least bit embarrassed about his shambles of an establishment, cheerfully crawled out the window of the room next door and into mine and let me in. I tried to call Sophie to report on the day's events but the phone didn't work, which at the Devonshire was often the case.

Once again, Cathy patiently suggested we fire Ornella and go through her agency, but once again, William and I were too smart to listen to her. Instead, we attempted to promote unity the only way we knew how: We threw a joint dinner party for the residents and the staff.

The guest list came to ten. Uniting the kitchen with the dining room was my childhood dream come true—and I was inflicting it on everyone. Who cared if my guests found the situation excruciatingly awkward? I didn't. I was overjoyed. Enacting my childhood fantasy of a big, happy interracial family, I set the table, laying on the good china, though the flat silver was just too much work. Dyed chrysanthemums in magenta, green, and blue (the only flowers left at the supermarket) constituted our centerpiece, and Afro-Cuban jazz grooved over the radio, courtesy of Edward. The couture ranged from Brooks Brothers to that Kmart line of sequined T-shirts (on Cassandra, not Mom).

William, wearing a black baseball hat and an apron, carved the roast beef, served with potatoes, gravy, and green beans. I herded everyone to his or her seat and bustled around, passing plates with a goofy smile stuck on my face. William lit the candles and the Reverend said grace.

"Shouldn't we be sitting in the dining room without *them*?" Walter asked loudly, glaring at the Reverend, who smiled at Walter in a very spiritual way. "What kind of party is this?" demanded Walter, looking at the multicolored faces around the table, his uncertainty and unease budding into anger before my eyes.

I stopped smiling, certain the whole happy tableau was about to blow up. "This is a different kind of party, Walter," Mom said, surprisingly coming to the rescue. I hadn't expected help from her corner.

"Oh," Walter said, miraculously satisfied by her answer. He looked back down at his plate. "Is that roast beef?"

"Yes, sir, it is," said my brother.

"Well, isn't that nice," Walter said. And that summed it up.

This party *was* different, and everyone was off-balance. But like strangers trapped in an elevator, we all did our best. For that evening at least, a truce was declared in the household. When it finally got going, the conversation ranged across many continents and touched on many ways of life.

"In my country," Edward said, "when a man is angry, the women kiss his feet and beg for forgiveness."

"Well, I wouldn't go that far," said Walter, "but it sounds pretty good, on the whole." Ornella, Cassandra, and I rolled our eyes and, smiling, shook our heads. Mom laughed, too, but you could see she didn't really catch on.

"In my country, when you get angry, you sharpen your machete on the front porch, where everyone can see you," said Cassandra, and she made a hissing noise, like running a stone across a blade. "When you get mad, you just murder somebody, ha, ha, ha!" A slight chill caught the back of my neck, right about where my head might get chopped off.

"In my country," Mother said, entering the conversation, "when you get angry, you say you are sorry."

"That doesn't make any sense," said Walter. "The person who *made* you angry should apologize."

"Not where I live," Mother said, glaring at Walter.

"I don't know what you are talking about," Walter said, and, demonstrating a textbook dementia symptom, removed a wad of chewed roast beef from his mouth and placed it in the little lineup of disgusting meat wads on the edge of his plate.

The harmony generated by our dinner party was short-lived. Mother and Walter continued to fight. Walter could be nasty or nice, and his unpredictability wore Mother out. One moment he'd embrace her, smiling, calling her "my Bride," and then suddenly pitch a tantrum because the phone rang and it wasn't for him or the coffee wasn't to his liking.

As if the voodoo problem hadn't been enough, another ridiculous plotline slowly emerged. Mother began hinting around that she had a "secret plan." Recalling Mother's other plan, the one where Walter would have a stroke, rumors of *any* plan were disturbing.

Mom's dementia was slippery. She might say one thing and then say just the opposite, in no way grasping the contradiction. Sometimes she could connect the dots and other times she could not. But, for the past month or so, she had been busy. Aided by Ornella, who thoroughly enjoyed her secret-agent role, Mother had made phone calls to her minister, her lawyer, and to Green Meadow, a classy old nursing home a few miles away. Her big plan was to drive up there and dump Walter at the front door with his bags—which didn't sound like a very well-thought-out plan to me.

Cathy often took Walter to New York for various medical and dental appointments. She used it as an excuse to pry Mom and Walter apart, and to have a day away from her kids. A rented limousine neutralized any arguments she and Walter might have over driving and parking. Later, she and Walter could enjoy lunch together without my mother needling both of them into a fight. On this particular drive, as Cathy relaxed in the plush backseat, her cell phone rang. Mom's lawyer informed her that Mom did not want Walter to live with her; in fact, she didn't want Walter in the house ever again.

Somehow, the Green Meadow part of the plan was omitted, which was probably just as well.

"Oh, boy," Cathy said. "There goes my day." And she told the limo driver to turn around.

Walter could not believe that his Bride was kicking him out. In a moment of penetrating lucidity, he demanded to be told by Mother, not on the phone but face-to-face. Then everybody went crazy making millions of phone calls: Cathy calling on her cell from the limo, William calling from Colorado, and the lawyers whipping faxes back and forth. Roland, en route to a business meeting, chimed in from an airplane. We were all thrilled with this development. Here was a simple solution to the hysteria and police visits, an end to the anxiety and abuse. An end to knowing you were failing to protect your mom (even if she wouldn't let you). Why, Walter could live with Cathy. What a great idea!

Ornella, under Mom's alleged orders, packed Walter's suitcases, set them by the front door, and waited for the imminent showdown. Alice, though swamped at work, was pressed into service. She canceled a client meeting, ran out of her office, jumped into her Jeep, and raced toward Oldhill on Route 46. Cathy and Walter held on tight while the chauffeur floored the limo, hurtling down Route 3 in the fast lane. As fate would have it, there was a crash on Route 46, causing a massive traffic jam, and Cathy and Walter beat Alice to the house by fifteen minutes.

By the time Alice galloped in the front door, the showdown was over, and Cathy was gliding out to her car.

"Addie changed her mind," said Cathy in passing. "A good old husband-and-wife communication problem. Whew, what a day! Bye."

A stunned Alice lurched into the living room, where Addie, red-faced and agitated, sat on the couch with Walter, who was oblivious to the proceedings. Ornella scowled and shook her head in the background.

Mother gave Alice an angry smile, the one she wore when suffering defeat.

"I never said I wanted Walter to leave," she said as Alice glared with disbelief.

"Are you saying you never told the lawyers, me, William, or Meg that you wanted Walter to live elsewhere, starting tonight?" said Alice, struggling to retain her balance even as the rug was yanked out from under her feet. "All this jumping through hoops to help you was for nothing?"

Mom's bottom lip trembled. "It was all a big mix-up," she said.

"Addie, we've got company!" said Walter, suddenly noticing Alice. "Say, I'd love to offer you a drink," he said, "but we seem to be out of the offerings. Maybe you could take me to the liquor store."

Alice burst into tears and stormed out, while Walter, serene as a cloudless summer day, ambled off to watch TV.

Ornella unpacked Walter's clothes while Edward laughed at her.

William was so disheartened, I didn't hear from him for a week. And each of the lawyers, Walter's and Mother's, sent a bill. In the face of this current conflict, Cathy suggested that Walter and Mom get some marriage counseling.

When the dust settled, it was hard to figure out, exactly, what had happened. Alice felt manipulated and betrayed. William believed Cathy and Walter bullied Addie into recanting. And from Roland's lawyerly perspective, it was Mother's frailty in the face of opposition, not any change of heart, that led to her infuriating reversal. His was a judicious, kind, and equally infuriating assessment, as no one was left to blame. It would have been very satisfying to point a finger and scream.

We were back to square one. Walter wasn't going anywhere. Addie, so shaken up by these events, had a mental remission and hardly made any sense at all. Even though weeks had passed by the time I next arrived for my week of duty, she was still staying in bed.

"There's some kind of wild thing," Mom said to me as she lay quivering under the covers.

"There isn't."

"I can hear it."

"There's nothing there."

"It is gnawing on the leg of the bed, and so are all the babies."

"What does it look like?" I said.

"Gray, with a long nose, a worm for a tail. Teeth." Her eyes widened. She was scaring herself.

"It sounds like a possum, Mom. Remember that time the possum got trapped in the basement wall? That was a very long time ago." The poor possum died in there with her family and made the whole house smell. But Mom would not stop until I crawled under her bed with a flashlight.

The peaceful if slightly morbid atmosphere of the Devonshire was a welcome escape, where the unwritten motto was "Why bother fixing anything when every repair is temporary?" I agreed. We're all doomed to extinction, so you might as well relax. That's how I felt about the ceiling repair in the decaying bathroom: a huge pregnant bulge right over the tub, secured with duct tape and looking like it might burst any minute. But who needs to bathe, really, when you consider the big picture?

One afternoon, William got a call from Cassandra. "You got a big mess here," she said. "Those people are robbing your mother blind." Every time Cassandra stocked the shelves on a Friday before going home for the weekend, all of it was gone when she came back to work on Monday morning. A twenty-pound box of laundry detergent disappeared, as did bags of flour, frozen meat, and loaves of bread. I questioned everyone. None of the staff knew anything, though Ornella accused Edward of stealing, and he returned the favor. My meals were disappearing from the freezer, but, based on the evidence, Mother and Walter subsisted on cold cereal and sandwiches on the weekend. "When I'm not here," Cassandra said, "your parents get nothing to eat."

That made me really mad. I was willing to feed my children tuna noodle in Halifax so I could cook nourishing dinners for my parents in New Jersey. But I was *not* willing to feed people I didn't know my beef stew, my meat loaf, and my secret recipe for corn pudding! Especially when Addie and Walter were therefore going hungry. And more than food was missing. The stainless-steel cutlery had been pilfered. All the good knives were gone, too.

Daisy corroborated this testimony. "Yes, that Ornella is a nice girl, but it is just too easy, you know, for people to start taking advantage." It was my fault. I should have had a locked pantry. Really, I had no one to blame but myself because it had never occurred to me that this kind of stuff was worth stealing. But of course a bag of sugar was, if you couldn't afford it in the first place. It was my fault for not keeping track, and stupidly putting people in temptation's way.

"What were we supposed to do? Lock up the food?" William said. "Don't be idiotic. We're doing the best we can. It's just that whatever we do, we make things worse, and Mother wouldn't want it any other way."

He had a point. We hired a plane; it broke. We put Mom in a nursing home; she left. We hired Ornella, and ended up paying the Reverend to protect the staff from one another, while the clients got robbed.

And so we fired Ornella and her minions. We didn't want to make it too obvious to Mom that we were calling the shots, so we concocted a plan that involved Cassandra taking Mom to get her hair done. But Mom smelled a rat and, at the last second, refused to go. Nevertheless we summoned Ornella to the sun porch, where a month earlier I'd fired Astrid, and closed the doors.

Mother lurked on the other side of the glass doors, forgetting we could see through them. William wimped out and I had to do all the talking. Of course, I had already cut my boss-lady teeth on poor old Astrid, whom I'd never wanted to fire in the first place. I began, "I'm sorry, but," when Ornella, her face all crumpled up, said, "I knew it!" I handed her the box of Kleenex. Ornella wept and Mother, watching through the door, began stamping her feet, filled with frustration and fury. Mother kicked the door before Cassandra managed to lead her away.

"Please don't go on the agency like Cathy wants! Miss Addie would be better off back in that home! Those agencies just hire any trash," Ornella wailed. (I did not point out that, originally, Ornella came to us, via Cathy, through an agency.)

We'd heard a lot of terrible things about agencies. "They hire anybody," the Reverend told us. "The agencies recruit in jails. They say they got clean people, but how do you know? You don't know who's in your house!" Of course, no one even bothered to lie to me about the Reverend's credentials.

The Reverend and Ornella quickly pulled up stakes, but not before Ornella slipped back into the house to cry all over Mother, who was totally demoralized and wanted to write her a big check. I interceded, as I had already written her a big check, and Ornella left in shame and defeat.

Then it finally dawned on me that Ornella, way back when, just may have been the one who engineered Mother's exit from The Glades nursing home. Certainly, she had plenty of motive. She took one look at Mom and smelled opportunity. Plus, she had plenty of friends who'd love to work under the table for her. Furthermore, if Ornella was the boss, she could claw back half her staff's pay.

And it was the Reverend, I found out later, who had instructed Ornella to fire Astrid. He divined, through his special psychic powers, that mousy old Astrid was scheming and employing evil spells to steal Ornella's job. The thought of Astrid doing voodoo on her must have scared Ornella to death.

After we got rid of Ornella, the immediate crisis dissolved. Mom stopped talking about getting rid of Walter, who calmed down a bit without Ornella around to snipe at him. Cassandra not only cooked and shopped, but cleaned, and did most errands so William, Alice, and I no longer had to—though, naturally, new complications arose to fill the void. Within a week, we signed on at Cathy's agency, and instantly we were involved with a whole new cast: Murbeth replaced Ornella as Addie's attendant, and as part of the deal, Cathy replaced the odious Edward with the shy but hilarious Jeffrey. Marilyn McClain, the agency supervisor, showed up regularly to check on Mom and Walter, and to snoop around and settle any issues with the staff. Life gained a modicum of predictability, at least during the week. But the weekends in the Departure Lounge remained an unbelievable mess. To her credit, Ornella had never left a shift uncovered, which is more than I can say for the agency. And money kept right on going out the window.

Chapter Four

PASS THE SAUCE

On the weekends, chaos and confusion reigned in the Departure Lounge. The regular staff people got a couple of days off, and the slots were filled with temps, innocent women who expected to prop the senior citizens in front of the TV for the day, heat up frozen dinners, then put their clients to bed. Little did they know. Agatha, though useless, was still on board as Walter's weekend helper. But Althea, Audrey, Dorothy, Jean, Maria, Flora, Alicia, and others all new to us, did time on Mother's payroll.

Church in particular was a major destabilizing event in our private little institution. Like a house of cards, a lot of shaky propositions had to hold up for Mom and Walter to get to church and back. In fact, I had to enlist Cassandra as the weekend chauffeur. In the best of all possible worlds, a perfect Sunday might look like this:

Let's say that Agatha wakes Walter on time. Althea brings Mom her nasty instant coffee, washes her, dresses her in a not-too-kooky outfit, and prepares a breakfast that she has time to eat. Walter, knowing he is going to church, dresses appropriately, gets his hair all Brylcreem-ed up, and consumes the waiting bowl of cereal without incident. Let's pretend the sun is shining and that Cassandra's car doesn't break down on the way to Mom's house, and that cats and dogs control the Nikkei exchange.

Keep pretending. Cassandra loads Mom into the front seat. Agatha and Althea are stationed in the back with Walter wedged between them, and Mom's walker is deposited in the trunk. The modest Church of Praise is a half-hour drive, if Walter doesn't take a fit and try to climb out of the moving car (which is why he is jammed in the backseat on the hump). Cassandra pulls up to the church, jumps out, retrieves the walker, and hands it off to Althea, who positions it by Mother's door before Walter escapes from Agatha and tries to help Mother himself. Today, Cassandra beats Walter to it, and the group makes it into the church unscathed. Walter helps Mom with her coat, almost knocking her down, and the old people are settled in their pew, fussing with their programs.

Cassandra and Agatha sit behind them while Althea retires to the parking lot to smoke. So far, so good.

After church, however, Mom and Walter want to go out for lunch. One memorable Sunday, they patronized the Cottage Kitchen, a venerable family restaurant with a bar. The dignified old couple—Walter in his camel-hair coat, Mom in her mink and church hat—stood in the queue, ignoring their trio of minders. Before Cassandra could cut him off, Walter pounced on the maître d'. "Excuse me, a table for two," he said, creating the impression that the three women behind him were total strangers. Unless Cassandra wanted a shouting match right then and there, she could only watch the lovely old couple hobble away, nodding and smiling without a backward glance. The SWAT team was promptly seated on the other side of the restaurant, out of range.

You won't be surprised to learn the day ended badly.

Mom and Walter had three rounds of drinks before Cassandra tipped off the bartender. "Water those down, unless you know CPR."

Agatha, Althea, and Cassandra were tucking into the huge plates of shrimp, chicken, and steak that Cottage Kitchen is famous for, when a familiar shouting erupted across the room. Walter, detecting the fake martinis, blew up at the waitress, calling her a "goddamn cheat." Mother's shushing infuriated Walter even more. He jumped to his feet, knocked over his water glass, and yelled, "Shut the hell up! Who asked you?" and slapped Mom's arm before a horrified audience. The dining room fell silent.

The manager escorted Walter out the door. Agatha and Althea followed, quivering so badly Althea could hardly light her cigarette, while Cassandra managed a weeping Mother. "Do not bring them back here," the manager told Cassandra. "They are banned!"

I know all this because the manager got my number from Cassandra and called me on Monday morning. I don't think a "ban" is something you can legally enforce, but Addie and Walter weren't going back to the Cottage Kitchen anytime soon.

In my parents' day, the elite were required to drink, to drink a lot, and to handle it. Only oddballs didn't drink. My parents subscribed to the "bum" definition of alcoholic. Alcoholics were drunken bums, men who'd lost their jobs and families, and lived on the street asking for handouts. If you had a drinking problem, but you weren't a bum, it's unlikely you'd be able to self-diagnose—because if you weren't a bum, you couldn't be alcoholic.

The servants were another story. As tradition decreed, uncles, aunts, nieces and nephews, and my one living grandmother gathered on Christmas morning in our dining room to eat croissants and drink coffee before opening presents. To serve this meal, Emma appeared in a white long-sleeved uniform and Tierney, who worked for both of my uncles, wore a white coat, black bow tie, and black pants. It never occurred to me as a child to wonder how they felt about going to work on Christmas morning. They'd always been there, smiling and saying "Merry Christmas" while serving orange juice and clearing away dirty plates.

One particularly memorable Christmas, Tierney staggered around the table with the uncanny grace that keeps a drunk upright. "More coffee, Miz Hen?" he asked my mother with a heavenly smile. Then, missing the cup entirely, he poured a steady stream of coffee onto the carpet. My mother narrowed her eyes, while my father hid a laugh in his napkin. The children caught on and pretty soon the whole table was roaring. My grandmother said, "Tierney, I think you are missing the cup."

Tierney watched himself pour more coffee on the rug, "Why, so I am, Miz Grandma, so I am," he said, laughing along with the rest of us, except Mom, who was furious. Emma came banging through the swinging door with a plate of hot rolls. She assessed the situation, took the coffeepot away from Tierney, and said, "You come with me." Tierney disappeared until Addie's ire died down and the inconvenience of his absence overcame her righteous indignation. Perhaps Tierney didn't mind spending his Christmases helping us celebrate ours. But the need for a couple of stiff drinks to face our Christmas indicates otherwise.

But Emma was a different story. She had a huge, sloping bosom, pale-brown skin, and the eyes glinting behind her wire frames let you know she didn't like children all that much. She had relatives in Maryland, but in Oldhill she lived alone in one room, with a fridge, a stove, and a window filled with plants grown from cuttings she took from specimens at our house. Stacks of paperbacks were piled high along one wall. Emma was dry and ironic, too smart to spend her life being someone's cook. I know this because for a few years, when my parents were off traveling, she and I spent a lot of weekends alone together.

Emma was originally hired to tend to my dad's invalid mother, Grandmother Henry. The private nurse kept her quiet with huge doses of morphine, but Emma caught on, and the nurse got fired. Thanks to Emma, Grandmother Henry regained her lively, good mind and enjoyed a few more years of life, with Emma as her steadfast companion. Grandmother was an opera lover; Emma loved baseball. Eventually, Emma became devoted to Puccini, Mozart, and Verdi, while transforming Grandmother into a Brooklyn Dodgers fan. They made quite a racket, hunkered down in Grandmother's bedroom with the radio blasting, cheering loudly through the baseball games and weeping and clapping through operas. After Grandmother died, Emma cooked for each of the brothers' families, and finally ended up working at our house. She watched fifteen grandchildren grow from babies into adults, went to their weddings and funerals, and witnessed batches of great-grandchildren come along.

In later years, Emma started showing up for work fortified with more than breakfast. Mom sent her off to rehab, and then gave her one more chance, or else. "I won't have it," Mom said, as though drink were a sin with which she herself was unacquainted. One day, Emma crept into the study behind me while I was making a phone call. I turned my head and caught her, dust rag in one hand and a bottle from the bar in the other, swilling it down. "Please, Emma! Don't!" I blurted out. I didn't want her to lose her job because I didn't want to lose *her.* Emma put the bottle down and with one hand on her hip said, "Don't what?" She knew I would never tell.

The really weird thing was, I'd caught Uncle John with the same bottle in his mouth, and he also knew I wouldn't tell. I was brought up to never "notice" such indiscretions, let alone mention them. This double standard prevented me from questioning my parents' drinking, and perhaps prevented my parents from seeing their own habits mirrored in the drinking spells of those they employed—the help, after all, were apprehended drinking on duty, at work! You can't drink on the job! How one drank *off-duty* was not under the spotlight, especially back then.

Mom lost her grip slowly as I grew up. The really hard drinking and bizarre stuff didn't start until I was a teenager, when I got mouthy and combative. I enjoyed making Mother, so proud of her decorum and self-control, sputtering mad. One night when I sneaked in late, every drawer in my room had been dumped on the floor, the clothes pulled from the hangers, and the bedclothes ripped off, exposing the mattress. Even my bookshelves had been ransacked. I thought we'd been robbed and went hollering into my parents' room, where they were in bed with the lights out. Mom said, rather thickly, "I was looking for the Scotch tape." That was all she had to say about it, but I knew her outrage had little to do with any tape.

Still, no matter how infuriated she was, she must have been loaded to go on that blatant rampage. In the morning, when I confronted her, she burst into tears.

By the time my comments had run through the family spin cycle, I'd been deemed unforgivably rude and cruel. Noticing that a person, let alone your mother, drank too much was a hurtful insult rather than the identification of a problem. "You made your mother cry," Dad said. Needless to say, it was a touchy subject, and none of us kids were brave enough to take it on again. And apparently it was none of our business.

But now it had become our business to tell Mom to stop. I could give her plenty of good reasons to quit drinking. It was bad for her brain and bad for her heart. One martini made her wobbly and two made her fall down. It encouraged shouting, public displays, trips to the ER, and hysterical phone calls—to say nothing of compromising the staff's ability to manage her. But the truth was, now I had a chance to punish her and I relished the opportunity, even though I pretended I was doing it for her own good.

At my prodding, Mother's doctors ganged up on her. "You might want to cut out the drinking for a while, until you're better," said a sympathetic internist, who adored Mother and was completely ineffectual.

"Now you listen to me and be a good girl," said the neurologist, who treated old people like imbeciles. "No more drinking! Ever again. No drinking at all. You be good!" If anyone talked to me like that, I'd get hammered at the first opportunity.

Finally, William and I lectured her, with slightly better results. "The staff is upset because it's their job to keep you safe, Mom," I said sternly. And William continued, "When you've had some drinks, you are much more likely to fall and break your hip." And the final big threat: "Then you will end up in a nursing home." Mom did not want to go to the nursing home. It was the only thing worse than not drinking.

We badgered her into agreeing and, with her permission, we emptied the bar. William and I even raided the basement, confiscating seven half-gallons of scotch, a case of red wine, two bottles of white, and three fifths of vodka, the result of Mom and Walter's clandestine phone campaigns.

Walter's Alzheimer's medication, if it worked at all, was undercut by alcohol, so Cathy didn't want him drinking, either. She found a special dementia doctor who wrote Walter an official note on prescription paper: "For the benefit of your health, do not drink alcoholic beverages of any kind." Walter kept this note in his wallet, and he often referred to it. "I do what the doctors tell me to do," Walter said, showing it to me. "I don't use the stuff any longer." Walter was content with ginger ale. As long as he had the note, he was as sober as you can be with no short-term memory. But Mom never gave up scheming ways to imbibe.

I was a total hypocrite. After a grueling day of home-care management, William and I, when we occasionally overlapped, repaired to the bar at the Devonshire Inn, worn out by our futile efforts to improve life for Mom and Walter. We got cozy on the chesterfield, gazing at the garage-sale portraits of those strangers we might have known but could not identify, finding relief in the warm alcoholic glow we denied our poor old mother. We drank until the portraits gazing back at us became awfully familiar, and ready to speak.

Enforcing the "no drinks" mandate was a lot like enforcing Prohibition. Mom was determined and sneaky. Walter, while he could remember that *he* didn't drink, couldn't get it through his head that his Bride was not supposed to, either. One day, Walter stealthily put on his coat and hat and tiptoed out the front door. Jeffrey caught up to him at the end of the driveway. "Mr. Huber, where are you going?"

"Goddamnit, I don't have to tell you," Walter said. And he went on his way, looking back and shaking his fist. To avoid detection, Jeffrey zigzagged among the rhododendrons and hedges that bordered people's yards, hoping no one called the cops. Thus Walter walked along—three blocks north, backtracking south, turning west, and going nowhere—with Jeffrey hopping from bush to bush, spying on him. At one point, Walter sat down on the curb.

"Are you all right, Mr. Huber?" Jeffrey asked, popping up out of nowhere.

"Where did you come from?" asked Walter.

"Oh, I was out for a little walk."

"You were, were you," Walter said, sitting with his long legs sticking out into the street, where they could get run over.

"Can you tell me where you are going, Mr. Huber?"

Walter got suspicious. "None of your business," he said. With Jeffrey's help, he got to his feet and ambled away, looking over his shoulder. Jeffrey waved to him until Walter quit looking back, and then Jeffrey resumed his covert operation. After a while, Walter slowed down again, uncertain of his route. Jeffrey caught up.

"When did you get here?" This time Walter was pleased to see a familiar face.

"Maybe I can help you."

Walter, who was tired of walking around, confessed. "My wife takes a little wine, and we seem to be *all out*!" He looked at Jeffrey, blinking a bit. Then, by way of explanation, said, "I don't use the stuff myself." Walter laboriously dug out his wallet for the note and showed Jeffrey the proof.

Jeffrey had a cell phone. In the end, Cassandra picked them up and rather than get into a fight, took Walter to the liquor store. There, not satisfied with just a bottle, he bought a case, so if someone dropped in, Walter could be a proper host. "I like to offer visitors a libation," he said. Walter, satisfied with the bottle in his hands, forgot about the case, which Cassandra returned to the liquor store later that day. She didn't even have to lug the box into the house.

No one had showed up at the house for a social visit in months. Walter did scare people away, but I think his temper was also a convenient excuse. If you cared about Mom, you could put up with Walter for half an hour. But it's my observation that old people don't really like to visit other old people with dementia—unless the visiting friend is younger. As long as you are younger, even by a year, you can think of the afflicted as a poor dear thing, *so* much older than you. Otherwise, it's just too frightening.

Before she finally married Walter, Mom often thought of dumping him because he humiliated and frightened her with his fits of temper. Of course she never did, but I was always hopeful that maybe she'd get unencumbered and move to Halifax. I was worried she'd end up lonely, rattling around by herself. Wouldn't she be much better off living close to me and my brother Roland? I fantasized about her loving it. She did, after all, love the "out of doors" in civilized doses. Surely she'd enjoy the graveled paths of Point Pleasant Park, with its acres of trees and meadows bordered by ocean, and the English-style Public Gardens, full of giant rhododendrons, formal beds, and swans. Her cultural interests would be fed, if not satisfied, by the Nova Scotia symphony and Neptune Theatre. And, for God's sake, she could always leave, vacation someplace—say, West Palm Beach.

When a fancy condo on my street came up for sale, I scoped it out with Mother in mind. I imagined our new life: the two of us sitting together, cozily installed in the pleasant living room, a cheery log on the fire, my children doing their homework at *her* kitchen table. A loving, multigenerational family!

Among the many things this utopian reverie ignored was the fact that Mother would rather die than move. I was naïve enough to send her a floor plan—and more naïve still to be crushed when she replied, "Move to *Halifax*?" as though I were suggesting she move into a crack house.

After Addie's stroke, a move was out of the question, even without the Walter factor. But breaking free of my Halifax family orbit to attend the inmates at Departure Lounge was getting harder with each trip. Prior to my departures, I cooked and froze the dinners my family would eat during my absence, washed everyone's clothes, made certain the carpool was driven by friends, and put a babysitter on call for loose ends. I left an hour-by-hour schedule for each family member, down to the dog. I ensured that all bases were covered, even double-covered with contingency plans, but Rob was a problem.

You could say my husband dislikes change. Using a new brand of laundry detergent sets him on edge, so my comings and goings threw him into hyperventilating panic. "I can't understand any of this!" he'd say, shaking my six-page, annotated family schedule, complete with flow chart, calendar, and menus. "How will the girls get home from school? What if they get locked out? What if they forget their lunches? What about soccer? What if I work late? What if the dog gets lost?

What if there's an *accident*?" Deep down, I think he believed that if he just made it hard enough, I would stay home.

So I dreamed up a new plan: *We'd* move. A New Jersey prep school was looking for an English teacher, and to my astonishment, Rob said, "Go for it." After three interviews and two days of test-teaching, I landed the job. I was ecstatic. It didn't pay all that much, but there was a great tuition break for the kids. I even found a house nearby, not quite as nice as ours, but bordering a gorgeous suburban park with soccer fields, tennis courts, even archery—all within walking distance of Addie. And Rob's employer had a branch in Parsippany, a workable commute. It was all falling into place!

The bubble burst when Rob said flatly, "Look, honey, I'm sorry, but forget it. This is a nightmare. We have a life *here*. We don't need a different life, and we are not leaving."

I had a little moment, like hitting the Pause button: Everything stopped and I dissolved into tears. Why, I demanded to know, had he not said so when I applied for the job? "I really hoped you wouldn't get it," he admitted, albeit sheepishly.

I was furious, spewing lava-like outrage—but secretly, I had to admit, if our roles were reversed, I'd probably have done the same.

I never told Rob this. A little leverage always comes in handy.

Dates don't matter much when the schedule that drives you is irrelevant to month and season. My shifts blurred together. I lost track of my trips, and what crazy things happened exactly which time I was there—it felt like I was always there.

On one shift or another, the taxi that brought me from the airport was still backing out of the driveway when Mom cried through the screen door, "We are going to Elizabeth Arden!" In the dimly lit front hall, her halo of wild white hair stood on end. Well, I thought, perhaps the world-famous Elizabeth Arden beauty salon on Fifth Avenue could get that hair under control.

As I bumped my bags through the door, Mom lurched toward me, and I caught her in a rapid embrace. Murbeth hovered from behind, her arms forming a protective arc in case Mom's legs suddenly gave way. I outweighed Mother for the first time in either of our lives, but I still wouldn't be able to hold her if her legs buckled.

"Yes! We shall become beautified at the Arden place!" Mom said loudly into my ear as she hung on to me. "And we will go on to the University Club for lunch." Mother's eyes blazed with anticipation. I shuddered. Fifty-fourth and Fifth, the location of our dual destinations, was Mom's old stomping ground, and part of her believed that if she returned to these shrines of beauty and power, she'd regain her former indomitable self.

"How were you planning to get to New York?" I asked as the three of us lurched toward the living room couch.

"I don't know," Mom answered with surprise, as if this were an entirely unexpected consideration. Murbeth cantilevered Mother into an upright position on the sofa and propped her up with a large cushion. Mom did not look directly at me, but I'd gotten used to it. She could see better when looking sideways.

With the confidence of a queen who knows her subjects will do her bidding, Mother said, "It will all be arranged." Murbeth, beyond the ring of Mother's vision, scowled. I didn't have to be psychic to get the message.

One of the great things about Mother was that, even though she was going blind, had stroke damage, lived with Mr. "Nobody told me!" and was a bit daffy herself, she was still cooking up schemes. And every expedition spelled disaster in one form or another. If I gave in to the impulse to snuff out her plans, she and Walter would never go anywhere. I had spent enough backbreaking hours on the couch with her to experience the tedium of Mom's life firsthand. If she wanted to go to Elizabeth Arden, I'd help.

Any expedition required a helper for Mom, one for Walter, and a driver. With William and me tagging along, serious transportation was required. "For that many people, you'll need the stretch," Sheila at the Sunshine limo service told me. I imagined a nice staid black limo, with six doors and jump seats. It cost a fortune. I booked it.

With Mother listening at my elbow, I navigated my way through

Elizabeth Arden's switchboard, booked Mom for a hairdo, and called the University Club, which was across the street. "Make a reservation for four," Mom said, attempting to give Murbeth and Jeffrey the slip. Getting rid of those bothersome helpers who wouldn't even let her go to the toilet alone was the first step toward recovering her former powers.

"Aw, Mom, there's six of us having lunch."

Mom raised her eyebrows and pretended she did not know Murbeth was in the room. "I don't think the University Club serves black people," she said in a stage whisper. In her right mind, Mom would never have that thought. Murbeth rolled her eyes. You could brush off the feckless remarks of an addled old lady, but a little always got under your skin.

"Mother, they serve black people at the University Club. They would serve blue people if they existed. It is illegal and wrong not to."

"Oh, right-o," Mom said. *Right-o?* Where was this stuff coming from? Her random utterances were deeply unsettling to me.

I called the University Club and explained all about our dementias, our caregivers, and our need for accommodation on the part of the dining staff. A man's voice as smooth as shoe polish said, "Don't worry—we have many older club members, and we can take care of you." This reassurance almost made me weep with relief. Even when Mom and Walter weren't being all that awful, waiters were impatient, sometimes rude, or incredibly condescending. I didn't want to get banned from the University Club.

William flew in late that night. When I informed him of this spectacular plan, he ordered a double. "No ice," he said. William never took ice in his drinks, because according to his Chinese doctor, cold drinks were terrible for his health. If you happen to have quite a few drinks, all that ice could add up to significant damage. I ordered my drinks without ice, too, for the same reason. "And what is Walter going to do," William asked me. "Get a facial? A little Botox, perhaps?" I had forgotten about Walter. What were we going to do with him?

On the morning of the Great Excursion, Walter got up and did not remember a thing about this plan. "No one told me!" he said. "No one informed me of these ideas." When you talk to Walter, it's very bad to start with "I already told you." This phrase will not advance the situation. But Murbeth, preoccupied with dressing Mom, forgot.

"We told you yesterday!" Murbeth said irritably over her shoulder, as she struggled to get Mom's wobbly arm through the sleeve of her dress.

"I'll have you fired!" said Walter.

"Your wife is my boss. Only she fires me, mister."

"I'm going to smack your goddamn black ass," Walter advised Murbeth.

Murbeth's nostrils flared. She looked like she might dump Mother on the bed and walk out the front door. You can't get paid enough to take this kind of abuse. But moving on to the panty hose, she said, as though throwing down the gauntlet, "No, sir, you will not!"

Insults were traded until Walter screamed himself hoarse. To his credit, he did not hit Murbeth. Mother remained passive, a rag doll in Murbeth's arms, pretending she simply wasn't there, a tactic she employed with increasing regularity. Finally both Murbeth and Walter calmed down. Murbeth propped Mom into a standing position and fastened a gold circle pin on her collar.

Jeffrey was having wardrobe problems of his own. "You are going deep into white man's territory, Jeffrey," I said, "and you need a tie."

"I don't own a tie," Jeffrey said. "In this line of work, I don't usually need one."

I brought Jeffrey's tie problem to Walter's attention. "I have a lot of ties around here somewhere," he said, gesturing vaguely about the kitchen. Jeffrey led him to his bedroom closet, where Walter had an abundance of ties. The two men spent a happy interlude trying out ties, until they settled on one with bold red and yellow stripes that clashed nicely with Jeffrey's maroon shirt.

Walter was convinced the driver would think we weren't home unless he stood right in front of the house, so I waited outside with him. The sun was bright on the flagstone steps and a breeze ruffled the early buds. He turned to me, his eyes bulging with panic. "Where are we going?"

"We're going to New York, for a hairdo and lunch. Ask me as many times as you want."

"Ah, so," he said, nodding, digesting this brand-new piece of information.

"Look at that sunshine," he said.

"Yes, sir, it's very cheerful."

"Wow. And look at those clouds."

We took in the shining firmament until William, dressed extremely conservatively in black leather pants and a black cashmere topcoat, locked the front door and joined us in the driveway. Mom descended from the main floor to street level in the elevator, a device she'd installed for her crippled sister, never imagining she'd need it herself. She and Murbeth struggled out of the tiny lift and clomped out of the garage.

In her mink coat and black felt hat, Mother looked as proper as a finger bowl. She waved at me with one gloved hand and clutched her venerable alligator purse in the other. Then from behind her, Murbeth emerged wearing contour-hugging lavender leggings, a fake metallic Gucci bag, and pink Nikes. This study in contrasts is the kind of thing that makes my life worth living.

The limo arrived, tailpipe scraping all the way up the ninety-degree driveway. Rather than the staid, conservative vehicle I'd ordered, Sunshine sent a party wagon with wraparound lounge seating and a full bar. The long, skinny bar ran the length of the car on the passenger side, outlined with a flashing strip of neon light.

Unfortunately, there was only one door, forcing passengers to stoop low and scuttle toward a seat. In the excitement, yelling, and confusion that followed, we made a strategic error: We put Mom and Walter into the car first. The old people sat squished together on the short bench at the back, with Walter draped across Mom's lap, while the rest of us had to climb over his legs. Murbeth and Jeffrey have a combined weight of about six hundred pounds, and though the limo was big, it wasn't that big. First Jeffrey climbed in, his coat sliding over Walter's head. Then Murbeth heaved herself in, shaking her behind directly in Walter's face. "What was that?" Walter said, looking incredulously at the massive purple bottom vaulting past him.

"This is ridiculous," said William, who had no choice but to deposit himself into the tiny space left next to Murbeth. I aimed myself at a small corner next to Jeffrey. We were smashed in so tight we had to breathe in unison. Just like family.

"Say, that's a nice tie you've got on," Walter said to Jeffrey. "I like your style." The driver slammed the door shut and backed out, scraping all the way.

Murbeth beamed, thrilled to be liberated from another endless afternoon in the house, and with the prospect of a fancy meal before her. When she and Jeffrey first signed on, the fine-dining scene intimidated both of them. In a panic, Jeffrey would order the first thing on the menu just to get it over with. He then often found himself stuck with a tiny appetizer, only to wait for hours as Mom and Walter ground their way through a three-course meal. Murbeth, too, was originally inhibited by the tuxedos and extra forks. But those days were gone. Now if the soup wasn't hot, she sent it back. If the steak wasn't tender, that went back, too. "More ice in my soda, please, while I wait for that steak," she'd say. Pretty soon, Murbeth had the waiter scurrying around in a sweat, and she relished every moment.

The tree branches, visible through the limo's sunroof, were heavy with green buds. Soon, bright shining leaves would unfurl, dropping a carpet of yellow blooms all over the ground. The whole town would smell like green honey, and a rejuvenating buoyancy would lift even the most solemn hearts. As the car wound along the sunlit roads to the highway, Mother said brightly, "This is just like being in a hearse."

"No, it is not, Mother," said William. "The hearse won't have a sunroof, and you won't be sitting up."

"No sunroof?" said Walter, chiming in agreeably. "You don't say."

"Oh, look," Mother said, surveying the interior of our conveyance. "A bar." She wasn't too blind to locate that. If you, like my mother, believe that drinking is the only response to stress, this car was prepared for any emergency. Walter heaved himself into an upright position and tugged on the cabinet door, which didn't budge. He tugged again.

"Hmm," he said. "Doesn't want to open."

Mother's eyes gleamed as she fixed them on the many shiny bottles winking behind the glass doors. Walter kept tugging on the doors.

"Mr. Huber, they're locked," said Jeffrey.

"They are?" asked Walter in mid-tug. "What kind of a bar is this?"

"Not a very good one," Mother said, her hopes momentarily dashed.

Jeffrey smiled. When no one else was paying attention, he caught my eye and dangled the keys. Foiled her again.

We whipped through the Lincoln Tunnel in record time and headed across town. The driver lowered the partition and asked, "What's the plan?"

"The plan," I said, "is to avoid the emergency room and the police station."

"That's the whole plan?"

"Aside from finding a parking place, that's it."

We cruised down Fifth Avenue and rolled up to Elizabeth Arden's famous Red Door, which featured a massive doorman in red coat and top hat. To his undisguised wonder, all six of us, in our assorted ensembles and sizes, crawled out of the hatch and lined up on the sidewalk as he ceremoniously opened the door.

"Is *this* where we're going?" asked Walter, a little pale in the face. Suddenly he scooted for the Red Door with a pronounced shuffle and an alarming forward tilt. I ran after him. Then he jerked to a halt and turned. "Where's my Bride?" he demanded, his eyes full of slightly crazy concern and snorting a little, a sign that trouble was on the way. He raced back to the car. "These people are supposed to look after her. Well, sometimes their attention wanders." He watched anxiously as Murbeth helped Mother into the wheelchair and, thankfully, got her seated before Walter interfered. And he was satisfied for a few minutes by pushing Mom himself.

Elizabeth Arden was amok with female tourists from across the globe, hell-bent on shopping. As we crossed the threshold, a thick mist that smelled exactly like grape juice emanated from the perfume counter, where sales associates sprayed perfume randomly into the passing crowd and made Walter sneeze. Navigating the wheelchair across the crowded lobby was impossible. The phalanx of eager store clerks, scanning for prospective clients, gave Mom a cursory glance and directed their attention to younger, ambulatory prospects.

Mother, smiling wildly up at the faces around her, was invisible to the shoppers packed like sardines in line for the elevator. I fended off elbows and handbags that came perilously close to whacking her in the head.

The beauty salon was even more crowded, overrun with scurrying stylists and robed and toweled clientele. The blow dryers made the place noisy and hot, while hairdresser music thumped in the background. Walter, Jeffrey, and William were quickly cut off from Mother, Murbeth, and me. We left them hanging around a product counter, where a desperate salesman tried to interest Walter in hair products. "This gel offers you maximum control without stiffness or flaking," he said, holding out a silver tube.

"You don't say," Walter said thoughtfully. "You better talk to this man instead." He handed the tube to William, who politely passed the guy on to Jeffrey.

Murbeth pushed Mother right up against the black wall of the chest-high appointment counter, and she couldn't see a thing. Beauty seekers milling around, awaiting transformation with their hair in foil and rollers, bumped the chair and jostled Mom as they tried to get past. "And who is this?" the receptionist asked, peering over the ledge.

I awkwardly tried to get Mom involved. "Mom, you are booked with Mr. Anthony, right?" But Mom, belittled, had absented herself, pretending she wasn't there.

"Anthony, your eleven-thirty is here," the receptionist called out, pointing at Mom. A beautiful thin man in silk and velvet swooped over.

"What do you want done to her?" he asked me. I almost slapped him.

"My mother can hear just fine," I said. "Don't be afraid to speak to her directly." I glared at Mr. Anthony, who got the picture and squatted down to Mom's level.

"In for a little pampering? Would you like a few curls? Maybe a nice rinse to lighten things up? Something off the forehead, I think." His coaxing worked. Mom came back to life, batting her lashless old eyes at him.

"Do what you will, but take care you do not make me look like George Washington," she said.

"I'd never make you look like that old queen," Mr. Anthony said, and he whisked her away though a curtain, with Murbeth following behind.

Walter, meanwhile, closely attended by Jeffrey and William, did not want any hair conditioner. "Who are all these people?" he said angrily, gesturing to the shoppers around him. "What are *they* doing here?" he said, as though his private party had been crashed by free-loaders. "Bunch of *women*!" he growled. Three Chinese ladies out for a day of beauty turned to stare. He wasn't going to last at Elizabeth Arden. We had to get him outside before he pitched a fit.

I wanted to stay with Mom, but the salon was so crowded there was nowhere to wait. Jeffrey, William, and I hustled Walter out into the crisp air, hoping a walk would distract him. But we got halfway around the block, and Walter began to lean against the buildings with one hand for support. His shuffling steps got shorter and faster, his breathing became rapid, and his face turned dead-white. I was afraid he'd collapse. Then *he'd* wind up in the ER, for a change. There were a few chairs on the sidewalk outside a café, and I managed to get Walter seated before he crumpled into a heap. William ordered him a Coke, hoping the caffeine and sugar would revive him.

"What is that?" Walter pointed. I followed his wavering finger to the sidewalk, over the curb, to the gutter. "That red," he said. A scrap of paper the size of a large stamp was stuck on the asphalt. William retrieved the item under discussion. It was nothing, a piece of litter—a dry cleaner's red tag. But Walter held it in his fingers, stroking it, fully absorbed in silence for a long time. The street was unusually quiet. A bunch of pigeons landed and pecked around, jerking their heads as they searched out crumbs on the pavement. A truck rumbled past, and the pigeons scattered and flew off.

Walter, still stroking the paper with his fingers, drank part of the Coke. His face was rapt with tenderness, as though he were falling in love. Rarely had I seen an expression like that on anyone, let alone Walter.

"It's nice," he said, as if pronouncing a considered judgment. "Very, very nice." Smoothing it out carefully, he handed me his treasure. Slowly, the spell wore off, and Walter's face folded back into its familiar vacancy, tinged with suspicion.

We agreed that Walter should not drag himself one step farther. William flagged down a cab for the one-block ride to our hallowed destination, the University Club. I ran back across the street to Elizabeth Arden, where Mother was attempting to pay, waving her credit card over her head to get the receptionist's attention while Murbeth ignored her. Murbeth, her back to me, was animatedly chatting with a newfound friend. In every store, hospital, or restaurant, Murbeth found someone from Jamaica. And Mom often got parked on the sidelines while her conversation ran its lengthy course until there was the inevitable exchange of phone numbers.

I buttonholed the cashier, Mom paid, and we fought our way out. Murbeth pulled Mom's hat down on her head, so I had no idea what Mr. Anthony had accomplished. I could only hope he made her feel like a million bucks, because that's what this little outing was going to cost.

The University Club had the quiet, reassuring atmosphere of the safe-deposit vault of a bank. Our party proceeded slowly across the black-and-white marble floor in the rotunda, through the sedate yellow sitting room where I'd had afternoon tea with Mom after shopping trips, to the muffled green hospitality of the Dwight Lounge. The maître d' instantly identified us, which was very reassuring, until Murbeth and Jeffrey were whisked off to their own table behind a pillar. Mother, Walter, William, and I were escorted in the opposite direction, to a table for four. The Cottage Kitchen syndrome. Didn't anyone understand that if you showed up with helpers, you needed their help? I realized, with sinking dread, that when the nice man said, *We can take care of you,* he meant he'd seat Murbeth and Jeffrey separately. As if by magic, Mother's will had prevailed.

The luncheon was buffet. Mother needed my help walking to the table, selecting items, maneuvering the selected items onto her plate, and getting herself and the plate back to the table without falling down or dropping the lunch. William got stuck with Walter, who was scowling at the food. Jeffrey and Murbeth were not responding to my telepathic appeals for help. Murbeth was leaning forward, telling Jeffrey something funny, and he was shaking himself, laughing. I ground my teeth.

I hovered, ready for a fall, spilled food, or an explosive argument. Ever so slowly, the two old people teetered along, reviewing the platters of meats, the piles of salads, cheeses, soups, and breads. By the time we got back to our table, Mom had nothing but beet salad and deviled eggs. Walter had managed to give himself a lot of shrimp, which he didn't like, and pickles.

The waiter appeared, wanting to know if we were paying for Murbeth and Jeffrey like they told him we were, and insistently led William off to confirm these arrangements with the maître d'.

I left Mom and Walter alone at the table just long enough to grab some food, so I wouldn't faint from hunger before we got home. I bumped into Jeffrey, who bore a plate of roast beef, chicken breasts, quiche Lorraine, potatoes Lyonnaise, crabmeat, the aforementioned beets, creamed peas, and a roll. "Looks good!" he said as he lumbered away. I heard Murbeth say, "You mean you don't *have* any hot sauce?" to a cowering waiter.

No sooner had I sat back down at the table than Walter, poking his shrimp, said, "I didn't order this. I don't like this at all. I am not going to pay for this stuff. Let me get that waiter back here." Walter rose, tottering off in the direction of the kitchen. William was nowhere in sight, so I was obliged to leave Mother alone and run after him. By the time I'd gotten a hold of Walter and led him back through the buffet line, where he selected a lunch to his liking, Mother made her move. An empty glass sat before her, and a waiter glided up with another on a tray.

"Vodka on the rocks, madam," he said, placing the second round on the table.

Mom smiled at me triumphantly, held up her glass, and said, "To you, darling, and to such a happy day."

There was nothing to do but applaud.

Chapter Five

ADRIFT

I was apprenticed to Mother and Walter, the Masters of Falling Apart. Since Ornella had pulled up stakes and the new team had taken over, I did less cooking, cleaning, and shopping. Now I did more time on the couch. And let me tell you, cooking and shopping were a whole lot easier. We were on rubber time in the Departure Lounge. Each hour rolled out for sixty minutes, then bounced right back. And no matter how much time went by, you never advanced.

One morning, I sat in the kitchen with Walter, drinking a cup of the bad coffee I had come to endure. Murbeth marched back and forth with loads of laundry, her sneakers squeaking on the linoleum floor, and she muttered and sighed each time she went by. The patter of Jeffrey's TV was audible from the guest room that never had "guests" in it anymore. The glass breakfast table was still crowded between a bay window and the bar (which perhaps had stimulated Walter's earlier bouts of morning drinking before he got that miracle note from the doctor). Sunlight glittered on the lawn. Brown sparrows flew in and out of the limbs of the cherry tree, their yellow beaks trailing grass and twigs for their new nests.

Walter had dressed himself with care, but his jacket and pants were from two different suits and the effect advertised his confusion. With deep concentration and puzzlement, he stroked the hem of his green plaid jacket, where it met up with the blue plaid of his pants. The threads lined up, but didn't match. Walter scowled, trying to formulate a thought that disappeared before he could quite grasp it, like a bubble that gets bigger and bigger, then pops into thin air.

Slowly the bewildering nature of his experience revealed itself to me. In a nutshell, the fog had rolled in. He couldn't really see back to where he'd been in his life and he clearly couldn't see what lay ahead. And where he was right now didn't quite add up. Sometimes a landmark popped out of the fog, but before he could make a positive identification, it was lost in roiling, gray bewilderment.

Walter's mental coverage of ordinary events was full of gaps—gaps that made him unable to understand, for example, how on earth the *dirty* plate that went into the dishwasher could then come out of it *all clean.* Sometimes such an event delighted him; other times, he'd be disturbed. Unable to put his experience into context or words, he was oddly open, vulnerable, and present in the gap. I began to understand that reasoning was useless. Good old logic could no longer address the swell of raw feeling that overtook him with increasing frequency.

Walter stopped fussing with his inexplicably mismatched outfit and turned toward breakfast, carefully concocting a mélange of dry cereals, in a mysterious ratio, slopping a little milk on his place mat because his hands shook.

"I think the other is just the regular stuff. It's this here"—he pointed to the Raisin Bran—"that really gives it flavor." He ate with concentration, grunting with satisfaction at the end of each bite. "I love breakfast," he said, moving on to a slice of bread. "Especially this final part," he said vaguely, knowing this description is not quite right.

"The bread?" I asked, trying to help out. He looked thoughtfully at the slice of bread, and finally accepted my suggestion.

"Yes, I guess you could call it that," he said, struggling to spread a pat of hard butter and mutilating the slice into a shredded mess that he then enjoyed.

"I feel we are at the end of something," Walter said, looking down at his empty plate. "What is it that we are?"

Somewhere in there, his intuition was operating, collecting feelings and impressions, and firing them out into the fog like flares that burst into balls of light and then fizzled.

"We are at the end of winter," I said, knowing that weather was reliable mental territory for him. "Spring is almost here. It's getting warmer and the buds are beginning to grow, and the birds are back and very busy, too." A bird in the cherry tree squawked for emphasis.

"Yes, but with spring, winter is coming again," Walter said, looking very gloomy. More and more often this is the way our chats went. We traded words in a very general context. If taken verbatim, there might be no explicit meaning, but I was learning to tune into the feeling.

"Walter, you are right. Winter is on its way. But before the snow shows up, you've got a summer coming, full of roses." I happened to remember he loved roses. Our conversation broke off, because Walter was distracted by a couple of sparrows who set up a ruckus, fighting over the little white birdhouse in the cherry tree Walter gave Mother back in their courting days. Walter pushed his chair back and stood.

"It's a little late for that," he said, and shuffled off to find his Bride.

Coming up with diversions that both Walter and Mother could enjoy was formidable. My job was to promote a cheerful atmosphere of companionship, because left on their own, they ended up fighting.

Walter and Mom were on entirely different and mutually exclusive wavelengths. Walter had no awareness that Mom frequently was batty and spouting nonsense. Her mixed-up ideas made Walter anxious and, if unmitigated, led to bug-eyed ravings. Even on her reasonable days, Mother was unable to prevent herself from referring to stuff he couldn't remember, until he was frothing at the mouth. Neither one could make allowances for the other.

I sat between the two of them on the couch in the living room, with a stack of photo albums on my lap. Beige grass-paper and pale wood moldings gave the living room a substantial feeling. A red and yellow Persian carpet of rare size and antiquity glowed warmly. A riotous arrangement of lilies shed petals on the piles of books cluttering the coffee table.

We'd had our morning coffee and cookies, a little break that came a couple of hours after breakfast. This routine was a road sign that said, WELCOME TO THE MIDDLE OF THE MORNING. THE NEXT EVENT IS LUNCH. Breakfast, lunch, drinks, and dinner punctuated the hours, letting you know how many more you had to endure.

I had dug out Mother's white leather photo album, and we embarked on a tour of Wellesley College, in the late 1930s, with Mother as our guide. Youthful, freckled, she appeared with wavy brown hair and a smooth oval face, standing shoulder to shoulder with a simpering friend. They were both wearing jodhpurs.

"Mom, you still have those jodhpurs in your closet!" I said. She did, in fact, still have an old pair of riding pants, if not those in the photo. I guess she just couldn't admit she'd never get on a horse again.

"I was a riding instructor for a few years," Mom said, looking pleased.

"Ah, so." Walter squinted at the little black-and-white picture with concentration.

"Say, isn't that nice!" He ran his fingers around the edges of the photos.

There was Mom in braids and tights with the drama club, and Mom with the writing club, looking brainy. Mom put a name to every face, which was really amazing, considering her eyesight. It wasn't until we were on the last page and an unpeopled photo of a building that I caught on. "And that's me and Betsy Gadston," Mom said.

"Are you sure that's Betsy?" I asked.

"Oh, yes. I'd never forget that face."

There was no face. There was no Betsy Gadston or anybody else. Just a brick building and some big trees. Mom could have made up all those names. I'd never know, and neither would Walter. I guess there's no point in admitting you can't see when you are looking at a photo album. If you want to enjoy yourself, you may as well be inventive.

"Wow," said Walter. "Isn't that amazing." He was still running his thumb over the edge of each picture, where they were glued to the heavy album paper.

"Yes, it is," I said.

Mother smiled. She was having a good time in the company of her long-gone college pals, pictured or not.

Walter was still staring at the building photo. "That is really something. How do they get them so square like that?"

This remark was completely uncharacteristic. Walter never remarked on architecture.

"Do you mean the windows, Walter, or the way the doors are centered?" I asked.

"No, no," Walter said. He meant the *photographs*. He flipped back to the beginning. "They're all so square and exactly the same size." He turned page after page with wonder. "Look at them all! How in heck do they get them like that?"

"I did," said Mother, smiling with happiness. "I took all those pictures."

"Really? You don't say," said Walter, visibly impressed.

Mom didn't take those pictures, for God's sake. She was in them. I knew we had just lifted off, but I had no idea where we were going.

"Yes, I took them with the bottoms of my feet."

"*What?*" said Walter. He knew this was not reasonable.

"Yes, and then I put them in my belly button," Mother said earnestly. I had to head this one off. Walter might take Mom's belly-button assertion as a complete insult to his intelligence and our happy entertainment would end in ruin.

If you don't hesitate, sometimes you can zoom right over a speed bump like this. You just floor the engine and soar right over it. "They can really do amazing things with digital cameras these days, can't they?" I said.

"I don't know about that," said Walter.

"No," agreed Mom. "That's computer stuff."

It's the hidden material that really drains you. Sure, the tension of being on the alert wears you out in the short term. But every feeble-minded exchange between Mother and Walter was wired directly to my own sense of demise. I could almost feel my skin shriveling and my mind going slack. I could barely keep myself on the couch.

We moved on to one of Walter's albums: panoramic mountain views, fields of cows, and castles with driveways full of vintage cars that were probably new. I turned the pages and my stepsister, Cathy, smiled through the years, improbably clad in green lederhosen.

"Look, Walter—that's Cathy!"

"Really?" He looked carefully. "Who? My wife or is it my daughter?"

I took a closer look. Surely the shapely legs coming out of those lederhosen indicated a daughter.

"You must have taken a family trip."

"Doesn't ring a bell," Walter said.

"Germany, maybe?" I suggested, because Walter spent part of his childhood in Bavaria.

"I wouldn't know," he said. He turned the pages, barely looking at them, shaking his head. He stopped at a series of shots taken in a hotel lobby, where a much younger Walter in black tie stood on a marble staircase, looking down at a woman in a red evening gown. A chandelier dangled over Walter's head in another photo, as he held aloft a champagne flute to toast the pork-faced men surrounding him.

"I have a suggestion for you," Walter said, very seriously. "If you are putting together books such as these, get a black pen and write on the back what they are. I can't recall this journey." He sighed, flipping through the pages again with remorse. "That would have been a very good idea." I appreciated this helpful tip from the Other Side.

Walter examined the picture of Cathy very carefully, squinting and shaking his head. "I had more children," he said, deeply perplexed. He counted on his fingers. "The boys: Greg, Fred, then daughter Cathy." Walter shook his head. "I find only three," he said, holding his middle finger tightly, "but I feel there were four."

I hoped Mother didn't jump on this fresh opportunity to hammer the truth into Walter's head. Lucky for me, she'd momentarily tuned out, busily picking invisible threads off the arm of the couch and pursing her lips. Before her stroke, Mother was determined to force Walter to remember, as though by doing so, she could eradicate his dementia. She even drove him up to the graveyard and confronted him with the irrefutable evidence of his son Carl's tombstone. "I don't recall," he'd said.

Walter produced the little leather appointment book that fit in his shirt pocket. He had worn the gilt off the pages, thumbing through them when he got confused, as he was right now. In his tiny faint penmanship, he wrote what was planned for the days, weeks, and months. The names of his children and their addresses were compiled in the back. But if you forget someone, how could you look him up? And of course, the deceased were not listed.

I had known Walter's fourth child, Carl. We both had been compelled to attend ballroom-dancing lessons. These were horrible affairs, where we mimicked adult social behavior, the girls in prissy puff-sleeved dresses and white cotton gloves, the boys in junior Wall Street blazers and ties.

On Thursday afternoons, skimpy boys led uncooperative girls through wooden replications of the cha-cha in a threadbare ballroom. We were instructed by a venerable old socialite who was forced by her deceased husband's debts to instruct the reluctant and unwilling. Her wall-eyed spinster daughter contributed to this economic effort by thumping out medleys on an upright piano.

Carl Huber was memorable as the only tall boy. He was handsome, with Walter's even features and a wide, welcoming grin. He didn't smell bad, like a lot of the boys did, and he didn't make fart jokes—very popular with that age group. I knew Carl in the osmotic way that teenagers roaming around in groups know one another. I didn't hang out with him, but I said hi if I chanced to run into him, and so did he. Otherwise, he wasn't on my radar. The last time I saw Carl, he was drinking a beer in the parking lot of St. Mark's Church before the service.

In the years between our ballroom dancing and our high school graduation, the 1960s social revolution blew American family life as we knew it into smithereens. Instead of debutantes, the girls grew into unattractive feminists with no social graces while the boys became unpalatable, amateur radicals—at least as seen by our parents. Some of us lived long enough to grow up, but Carl died. The circumstances were vague—suicide, overdose, bar fight—and I never did learn exactly what happened.

Walter knew he'd forgotten something fundamental. But he couldn't even recognize Carl's photograph, and nothing in this world could bring Carl back. Due to Alzheimer's, Walter no longer suffered that memory, which some might think was a blessing. But to me, it seemed more like a curse. Haunted by the lost child he could not name, when Walter counted off his children, he inexplicably found one extra finger. No matter how warm the day, he shivered in the shadow of that phantom child. Such things are carried within us, deeper than memory and with no hope of resolution. I believed that even after Walter forgot everything—all of us, the four seasons, the whole blue and green world—that deep chill would pass over him.

"That is very, very troubling, Walter," I said, patting his arm. "But some things are just a mystery."

"Well, yes, a mystery," Walter said, sounding relieved. "I guess you could call it that."

As I saw into his illness, I became sympathetic. He may have been shallow and temperamental—opinions advanced by those who had known him. He certainly bullied my mother and threw tantrums and fits that made her life miserable. But his illness made him vulnerable, and I was guiltily growing fond of Walter. I made a point of being warm, nonconfrontational, and nonjudgmental, whenever possible. Inevitably he got worse. Over time, the inhibitions that kept tabs on his behavior disappeared into dementia, and he had no control over his aggression or, as it turned out, his lust. That's where my sympathy ran out.

There are some things a child shouldn't have to deal with, even as a grown-up. One of those things is your parents' sex life. When I was a child, I shuddered upon learning the facts of life. I'd vaguely imagined I was conceived through a telepathic mental process, not this implausible physical bumping and grinding that my respectable father and mother allegedly performed—for pleasure! There was nothing in their attitude, nothing in their opinions or comportment, to support the veracity of this claim. How freaky could it get?

The answer is, a lot freakier. As Walter's mind deteriorated, his private parts perked up. Thanks to an abundance of geriatric-health-aid catalogs, Walter could be considered armed and dangerous on that score. Cassandra said to me, "Walter gets a lot of packages he takes in his room, and you don't know what he is doing in there."

One afternoon, sitting around with Mom sorting the mail, I came across the Galaxy health-care catalog from Framingham, Massachusetts. On the cover was a cute gray-haired couple, the woman holding a bouquet of flowers and being pushed along in a wheelchair by a vigorous man, presumably her husband.

The products all look innocuous (until you imagine needing them yourself): the long-handled bath sponge, extra-long shoehorn, the pill pulverizer, the utensils with built-up handles "designed to assist self-feeders." There's everything imaginable to replace something you have lost, like use of your limbs. But the really scary stuff is in the back. I won't go into the details of the "erect aids," except to tell you that the cheaper one is around three hundred dollars, and you have to plug it in to make it work.

Apparently Walter had opted for a thriftier remedy the first time, from a fly-by-night, brown-wrapper mail-order company. He prowled around the mail slot for days. When his parcel finally showed up, he pounced on it and then ran to his room. A little while later, he emerged smelling strongly of peppermint, and attempted to lie on top of Addie on the living room couch.

It took everyone a while to put two and two together: When Walter smelled like a candy cane, he was in the mood for love.

Unfortunately, Walter didn't stop there. He devoted himself and his credit card to the pursuit of greater satisfaction. Within weeks, the mailman was lugging bags full of catalogs to our door, catalogs that made Victoria's Secret look like Beatrix Potter.

One catalog shamelessly frightened potential customers with nagging erectile dysfunction away from legitimate medication—*FDA reports over 20 deaths!*—toward the "Erectolizer." This remarkable contraption, which resembled a see-through bicycle pump, was offered in low-priced economy models all the way up to high-class versions decorated with chrome plate. Apparently, Walter was inching his way up to the luxury edition, and the mystery packages continued to arrive.

Cassandra, shaking with laughter, showed me a recently arrived sex-aid brochure. In the cover photos, a smiling old couple reclines on a blanket on a bright-green lawn, the remnants of their romantic picnic—cheese, bread, grapes, and wine—displayed around them. A vibrant older woman leans against her balding male companion as he tenderly strokes her face.

"What's wrong with this picture?" Cassandra asked me.

Aside from the fact that no one is really all that comfy sitting on each other like that, I didn't know.

"If her husband was trying this stuff out every night, she wouldn't be smiling!" said Cassandra. We both had a good laugh at Walter's expense, but as time went on, the situation became very unfunny.

Like many older couples, Walter and Mother had maintained separate bedrooms, but his renewed interest led him to her door. Almost every night, after the lights were out and Mom was asleep, Walter woke up ready for love. So he ministered to himself with his various mail-order devices and creams. Then, when his physical condition matched his desires, he ran into Mother's room and jumped into her bed. Mom was jolted awake by Walter, clutching, pawing, and moaning. Incapable of taking Mother's frailty into account, Walter didn't realize his insistent attentions were hurting her.

Mom's flaky mental condition was quite different from Walter's. Though her clarity was variable, she maintained enough self-awareness to feel degraded and humiliated. She dreaded going into bed, not knowing when he would ambush her. And though she complained and agonized to Cassandra and Murbeth about Walter's nocturnal visits, she never said no to him. Mother could not bring herself to refuse him, not that it would have been effective. I am pretty sure she was brought up according to the unspoken code of her day—namely, it's your duty to service your man. If you don't, he'll find satisfaction elsewhere.

"She isn't getting any sleep," Murbeth told me. "She's got bruises from his big old hands."

"Your mother is too fine for this kind of thing," Cassandra said. "Lock the man out! Put a lock on her door!"

"Put a lock on his door and keep the man in," Jeffrey suggested. The staff was disgusted.

The house was small. Murbeth and Jeffrey, who lived in during the week, were confronted with this occurrence nightly. They couldn't avoid knowing exactly what was going on. To many people, the image of a randy old man making love to his wrinkled, gray-haired wife is a distasteful setup for a joke—if not something even more distasteful. But it wasn't a lack of propriety that disturbed Murbeth and Jeffrey, straitlaced and God-fearing as they were. What upset them was that Walter was stronger than Mother, and he noisily climbed into her bed whether she wanted him there or not. Now I didn't care if Alzheimer's was to blame. I could not consider Walter with a shred of kindness.

Nobody told me I'd have to protect my mother—who never had a frank sex discussion with me in her life—from the inappropriate sexual advances of her demented husband. This was way out of my comfort zone. Every night, I lay in my own bed in Halifax, unmolested, safe, secure, and unable to sleep, knowing that Mom was being taken advantage of. I had to protect her, not that she'd ever say so.

On my next visit to New Jersey, I went over the situation with Mother, in fairly elliptical terms. "Mom, you seem so tired. You really need to get more sleep. I know that Walter has been keeping you up at night, but he needs to keep himself company until you get some rest." I fixed the lock on Mom's door, and I had a little chat with Walter about the birds and the bees—and how they need sleep, too. "You need a good night's sleep, Walter, and Addie needs her sleep. You don't want your Bride to be tired and run down, do you?"

"I always get a good night's rest," said Walter by way of reply.

"It is very important that you stay in your own room and let her sleep. Stay in your own bed."

"Sleep is very important," Walter said.

Well, that night he could not remember our civilized little chat.

"I want my Bride!" Walter demanded, throwing himself, kicking, against Mom's door. The yelling and battering increased in frequency and fury. Mother was frantic.

"Just let him in! Let him in!" she pleaded with Murbeth.

The phone rang in my decrepit room at the Devonshire Inn, waking me from a fitful sleep. By the time I got over to the house, still wearing my pajamas, Walter had taken a whack at Murbeth and someone, I can't remember who, panicked and called 911. More shouts and bellows ensued. Mother was out of bed, banging on her side of the door, shouting, "Let me out!" At one point Walter got his hands on the TV remote and was brandishing it like a *Star Trek* weapon. My attempts to intercede with calming, soothing dialogue were useless.

When the police showed up, Mother refused to make a statement against Walter. "Ma'am, do you want to file charges against your husband?"

"No, no!" said Mother.

For a very brief moment, while I was trying to explain, it seemed like I might get taken downtown for keeping two legally married people apart in their own home.

"Haven't we been called up here before?" one officer noted.

"You are wasting our time. Like I told you, put these people in a home!" said the other. They were both so young, their ears stuck out. Their parents were probably still fine and dandy.

In the course of these events, Walter and Mom had become united against the rest of us. "You want Walter to go to jail," Mother said accusingly. "Why would you do a thing like that?" Walter had gone blank, as he sometimes did. Totally baffled, he followed Mother down the hall. "You better come and stay with me tonight, Walter," she said as they got to his bedroom door. "I'll need help if the police come back."

"The police?" he asked. "Really?"

The whole thing was absurd, and I couldn't help feeling a little like I'd been framed. In spite of everything, I burst out laughing, all the way back to the Devonshire.

The next night we didn't bother to lock the door, and Walter crawled into bed with Mom, who complained bitterly the next morning to Murbeth that she'd rather die than have to put up with Walter. Rubber time at the Departure Lounge had me beaten again.

When I attempted to let Cathy know how bad things were, she

minimized the seriousness of the problem. "This is a major issue for oldsters," Cathy said. "It comes up in nursing homes all the time, the old characters hopping in and out of bed with each other! You should hear those stories!"

"Well, if I can't protect Mom, Walter will be in a nursing home!" I shrieked at her, even though I knew Cathy couldn't put Walter in a nursing home any more than I could put Mom into one—because our loony parents were "legally competent" until proven otherwise. Right now, I ignored that fact. "Or Mom will go, and then Walter has to move out!"

Cathy agreed to talk things over with Walter's fancy New York doctor, who'd successfully gotten him to remember not to drink. But I didn't think Walter's doctor would get the full picture from Cathy. I suspected she'd "minimize" Walter's problematic behavior, and I wanted to set that doctor straight myself.

My cell phone rang as I stood in the rain on a Nova Scotia soccer field, attempting to take down the nets. We'd lost the game in a shoot-out, and my daughter was upset. The doctor was at Mount Sinai hospital in upper Manhattan, New York traffic whining in the background as the cold summer rain pounded down on me. The girls jogged up and down the field, sloshing through the puddles.

"Wow, Nova Scotia—that's in Canada, right? I've always wanted to go there!" the doctor said.

"I need to get Walter out of my mother's pants!" I shouted, putting not too fine a point on the situation, as the line crackled and rain poured down the back of my neck. An eavesdropping soccer mom regarded me with alarm.

"Yes, I spoke with Cathy. We'll bump up Walter's medication. That should keep him in his own bed," the doctor reassured me. I was not exactly reassured, because Cathy was against sedating her father. We'd suggested it before. "I don't want to compromise my father's quality of life," she'd said.

I watched the soccer team across the soggy field while trying to concentrate on this disembodied and utterly bizarre conversation.

"You really need to insist that Cathy complies, because, frankly, if Walter can't be controlled, our living arrangements will collapse. I'm afraid I don't think my mother is Cathy's first priority." I assumed the doctor thought, as I did, that Cathy was obsessed with preserving Walter at any cost, especially my mother's. But the doctor's tone instantly went tart.

"Of course she's worried about her dad. She's just as worried about him as you are about your mother—and she is sick and tired of being threatened with nursing homes!" Wow. I was not expecting that smack-down. Suddenly, as if a jolt of electricity had jumped out of the phone and into my head, I saw Cathy as this doctor did—a worried and harried family caregiver doing her best. I swallowed hard and mumbled a good-bye.

I stuffed the wet nets into the soccer bag and lugged them into a car full of girls who were unaware of my unsavory, unsolvable problems. They were despairing over the tragic loss of their soccer game. So, with my stomach churning, I took them to Dairy Queen for a cheering dose of cheap fast food, which I was too upset to eat. Feeling bitter and angry was making me sick. I didn't even have the satisfaction of being mad at Cathy.

After some detective work, it became clear that Walter was up at night torturing Mom because he slept all day. Jeffrey liked to sleep in, so he didn't bother to wake Walter up until late. Then Jeffrey let Walter nap all afternoon, while he drank tea and chatted with Cassandra in the kitchen. All that daytime rest was fueling Walter's nocturnal activities. Now Jeffrey would have to work for a change. He'd have to get Walter up and keep him busy. No more sleeping during the day. No more naps for either of them.

Considering Walter couldn't cut his toenails without drawing blood, the doctor worried that Walter might injure himself with his inventory of complicated electrical devices. So Jeffrey spirited Walter's arsenal away. At first Walter sifted through his drawers, but eventually he forgot about it.

However, if the smell of peppermint wafted through the house, the staff got really nervous.

Chapter Six

DIGGING DOWN

There had never been anything easy about Mom. She had a lot in common with God, a confused, vengeful, Old Testament God who'd read Freud. Remember, Mom thought she could smite Walter with a stroke.

The two of us were at odds from the start. For one thing, we were dead ringers, twins separated by thirty-six years. So perhaps I'd always been a walking advertisement for the stuff she hated about herself.

I was barely out of the womb when she packed me off to live with a retired nurse for my first three months of life, because I didn't fit into the summer schedule.

"They didn't even want you," gloated Sophie, who at age six had been abruptly dethroned as Mommy's Baby Girl by a loathsome baby sister. She must have been thrilled when they left me behind. When I popped up at the end of the summer, she probably felt betrayed all over again.

Just before Mom got pregnant with me, it was her turn to take charge of my paternal grandparents' summer home, a fussy mansion on the Jersey shore. The junior female family members took turns overseeing the cooking, cleaning, shopping, menus, parties, transportation, and so forth. This permitted Grandmother and Grandfather Henry to reign over their dining room with its fancy marble fish pond, and their formal terraced gardens, complete with fountains and moss-stained statuary. "There wasn't room in the plan for a baby," Mom told me many years later.

"Your mother was nervous, you know," our housekeeper Millie said to me. "High-strung." But even if you're high-strung, getting rid of a new baby seems like extreme dedication to the plan, if you ask me. What would make you do a thing like that?

Dad was fourteen and a half years older than my mother. When they met, he was a divorced, middle-aged father with two children, and he was fully immersed in the family firm, a budding chemical company. She was a college girl writing book blurbs at Charles Scribner's Sons. The instant she married, she went from living the single life in New York to being a New Jersey matron saddled with a fully furnished household of servants, plus my half brother and sister, who had been doing just fine without her.

Dad's parents were proper Southern Baptist teetotallers, who credited God and clean living for their ascendance from a dirt farm in North Carolina to prosperity in New Jersey. My father and his two brothers drank and gambled. Well known at the racetrack, they made wagers, bets, and dares on everything from the number of crows in a tree to the number of bottles of gin they could steal from a bar. But these antics were kept strictly secret from their straitlaced parents.

I should mention that the Henrys were a formidable clan, well known around town. If you married in, you had to deal with all of them: Father and Mother Henry, Dad and his brothers, the sister, their spouses, and all the children. Thursday-night and Sunday-noon dinners at Father and Mother Henry's house were a requirement, not an invitation, along with birthdays and holidays.

My father was their eldest, a nerdy-looking kid with a big head and glasses, who graduated from Princeton at nineteen and, impressed by F. Scott Fitzgerald, wanted to be a writer. "My father had other plans," Dad wrote, and he ended up working for the family business for the rest of his life.

Dad married his first wife, Daphne, when he was full of beans and full of booze. She was a celebrated beauty, a good girl who was just a little bit naughty. Dad's sister fawned over her, his father doted on her, and his brothers drooled over her. But under the increasing responsibilities of the family firm and then fatherhood, Dad sobered up into a boring, stalwart citizen. And Daphne, stuck with tomato juice on ice before dinner with the in-laws, languished. She did not find the unglamorous demands of motherhood and household rewarding. At all. When she dumped Dad, the entire family considered themselves betrayed. They had taken her into the fold and counted her as one of their own. My aunt slashed Daphne out of all the family pictures, and the albums were full of severed photographs. Daphne might be gone, but her absence remained.

When Mom showed up years later, she was welcomed with some reservation. The Henrys were not about to be wounded again. Mother had to prove herself worthy. She had to become the unparalleled daughter-in-law, the best sister-in-law, the most gracious hostess, and the most trustworthy helpmeet, just to cover all the bases. She was so worried about any comparison with Daphne, Mom ditched me rather than let the family down, even a little, and tarnish her image. After all, Daphne was still out there living in Florida, and you never knew that she wouldn't somehow engineer a comeback.

Mother would run right over you if she felt she had to. I knew it, and she scared me. When I was three, she caught me playing with matches. Ironically, I was pretending to be her, powerful Mom lighting the fireplace. She grabbed my hand, lit a match, and held my finger in the flame until it blistered. "This is for your own good," she said, glaring at me. I learned nothing about the hazards of matches, which I already knew. But I did learn that Mother would go pretty far to prove a point.

Mother, perhaps needing time alone with Dad, had me put to bed at 7:00 P.M. and expected me to stay in bed until 6:30 the next morning. I used to lie awake for hours, rocking myself and singing, watching twilight disappear and the sky go dark. I got in the habit of turning on the light and creeping out of bed to play. The study where my parents drank and conversed after dinner was directly beneath my bedroom, so I tiptoed carefully to avoid detection. But one night I knocked over the lamp. Mother, bright with cocktails, charged into my room and caught me with a play stethoscope around my neck and broken glass all over the floor.

For a week, she tied my wrists to the headboard and my feet to the footboard with lengths of clothesline, much like stretching me on the rack. "You need your sleep," she said. It did not occur to her that I might not be capable of sleeping so many hours. Each morning I begged her not to tie me up again, but Mom was intractable. Frances felt sorry for me and tried to intercede. "Miz Hen, I don't know about this tying."

"When I need advice, I'll ask for it," snapped Mom. I overheard Frances say to Millie, "Acts like that child is a dog." How could you trust anyone who burned you with a match one minute and tied you up the next—all for your own good?

Mother ran our home like a naval vessel: breakfast at 7:30, lunch at noon, tea at 4:00, cocktails at 6:00, dinner at 6:30, every day. It never varied. You, as a member of this organization, were required to be in the right place at the right time, saying the right things and properly attired. Nothing was left to chance.

Every Monday morning throughout my childhood, Mother sat in the kitchen with a stenographer's pad and pencil, planned the week's meals, and ordered the groceries by phone. The cook consulted Mom's list and duly prepared the meals. In the evening, Mother and Father relaxed over cocktails while the maid in a gray silk dress and white lace apron set the big dining room table with flowers and candles, sterling and Spode. She then crossed the carpet to the threshold of the study and announced, with a little curtsy, "Dinner is served, Miz Hen."

Once we were all seated—hair combed, ties straight, nails clean—Mother pushed a buzzer under the carpet with her foot. Having spent my early years dining in the kitchen, I can tell you that buzzer was as loud as a fire alarm. The maid entered through the swinging door bearing first the roast, then the mashed potatoes, then the spinach. Finally our plates were full. The maid withdrew, and the swinging door swished closed. Mother said a quick grace and picked up her fork, signaling permission to eat.

During the meal, Mother played a little power game I call "Interrogation." This is a tried and true method of social intercourse that replaces conversation. The interrogator (a.k.a. Mother) almost never ventures an opinion of her own. Between bites of food, she questions the interrogatee, who struggles to manipulate the heavy silverware correctly while coming up with a satisfactory answer. As you floundered, Mother critiqued your table manners, pointing out your mistakes by flicking her middle finger sharply against the back of your hand, if you were within range.

Mercifully, the interrogation ended when Mom rang the buzzer for second helpings, then again for dessert. When these were gobbled up, dinner was adjourned, having required exactly twenty-five minutes from soup to nuts.

Afterward Mother sat in the study with Dad, rating the food, the service, and her children's appearance and behavior, while sipping coffee from a demitasse cup—provided by the maid, who then shed her uniform and left our house for her own. Our entire domestic life was similarly scheduled and executed, creating an orderly grid for all family experiences. It was a lot like being shredded on a cheese grater.

The dinner theater I endured growing up was barely recognizable now in the remaining ruins. Instead of saying, "Miz Hen, dinner is served," from the edge of the room with a ridiculous curtsy, Murbeth marched over to Mom with "Dinner ready, time to get up, let's go." Pulling her upright, she conducted Mother to the table. If Mother refused the walker, Murbeth grasped the waistband of Mom's pants. "Get away! Don't touch me!" Mother hissed, swatting at Murbeth's hands.

"I'm not going to let Mother fall again. Okay?" Murbeth said firmly as Walter fussed, grabbing at Mom because he wanted to be the escort. Murbeth deposited Mom in her chair and departed to her spy post in the living room, where she kept an eye on the dinner proceedings, which sometimes got out of hand.

A dusty silk tulip centerpiece was partnered with a lone candle on the table. Walter looked down at the meal, already portioned out on the plate before him. "What is this we're eating?"

Mother made a wild guess, because she couldn't see it. "Creamed chicken, I think."

"Creamed chicken? That's not any kind of creamed chicken!" Walter said, his tone escalating.

"I think it is!" insisted Mom, whacking the meat loaf with her fork. "Chicken!"

Walter roared, "That isn't any kind of goddamn chicken!"

Murbeth was on her feet, ready to run in and break up a fight, but Cassandra, who heard every word, blasted through the swinging door.

"That's chicken meat loaf, Mr. Huber," she said. "You are both a little bit right. Now eat your food." Mom and Walter cowered as Cassandra swished back into the kitchen.

Mother tapped the fork against the plate until she located a bite, and then attempted to skewer it. Unfortunately, most of the meal landed in her lap. There was little conversation, because Walter responded to Mom with "Who cares about things like that?" and there was no one else to talk to, unless I stuck around.

Mother summoned Cassandra by clanging the brass school bell that had replaced the buzzer on the floor. "Is that all you're going to eat, Miss Addie?" Cassandra asked, surveying Mom's plate. "Murbeth, why you not give Addie a spoon, girl?" Cassandra yelled to Murbeth, who was hiding around the corner. She put a spoon in Mom's hand, and Mother dutifully maneuvered food into her mouth, a slow and agonizing process.

Finally Murbeth swooped in with a damp washcloth and cleaned Mom's face and hands, scrubbing vigorously until she resisted. "Mother watch TV now," Murbeth said, propelling Mom into the TV room. Walter, grumbling but not boiling over, located *Wheel of Fortune,* and both of them sat there, mesmerized by Vanna White. Then Murbeth and Jeffrey put the two old people to bed, their last duty of the day—until the impromptu night happenings began, whatever they might be.

Mom was not having a good day. Her hands were battered from a fall in the night. Allegedly, she had tried to call Murbeth, who had failed to show up. Some nights Mother was up every hour, thinking she had to pee; chances are Murbeth pretended not to hear her. Mom had struggled out of bed by herself, teetered into the bathroom, and then fell, hurting both of her hands.

And allegedly Walter woke up, helped her off the floor, cleaned the blood from her cuts, and helped change her nightgown because Mom had fallen before she got to the toilet. Mother said, "He made things right." He settled her into bed, then climbed in on the empty side to comfort her. How they managed with the bed rails, I don't know.

Something didn't quite add up in this tender story, like maybe Walter showed up with something else on his mind. Maybe he pushed Mom, and that's why she was bruised. But what difference did it make? There was nothing I could do about it.

Whatever happened that night, Mom was rattled. She kept standing up alarmingly, as though she were about to go someplace—then thumped abruptly back down onto the couch. She picked at herself, opening scabs on her arms. And she was mentally incoherent, fading in and out like a weak radio signal. You got the thread of one story mixed in with words and phrases from some unrelated mental broadcast.

I dutifully sat on the couch with her while Walter looked at the paper. I don't think he read it, but he appeared satisfied turning the pages. Mom was telling me some crazy thing about Haile Selassie in exile. "They kept him in a cave, and brought him a harem of women in the dark," she said. "And he became a leopard." Loop de doop.

"I hope his girlfriends liked animals," I said.

"No, they didn't," Mother said firmly. "They wanted him to die, so they could have the limo."

"What limo?" asked Walter, perking up at the mention of a subject he could appreciate.

"The one Sophie got us," said Mother.

"*Sophie* got us a *limo*?" said Walter. "I don't recall."

"Yes, that time in Florida, when I had my fall," said Mother, who turned toward me and in a confiding tone added, "I'll always be so grateful for everything she did for me."

"Sophie did not go to Florida, Mom. That was *me,* Meg," I said. I was the one who changed your diapers and rented the plane. I'm the one who cried and wrung my hands for you, not her! "Mom, Sophie was not there."

"No, no, darling. You are the one who's here now. She came all the way from California."

I wanted to scream.

My sister laughed when I told her. The shoe had been on the other foot plenty of times.

Mom loved us, but you had to be careful, because she was big on conspiracies. She didn't know how to evoke intimacy without uniting against a common enemy. And so she'd make just the two of you (you and Mom, that is) into "us" against "them" (your loving siblings). Most of her jokes were at someone else's expense, and you found yourself inexplicably joining in, making witty, cutting observations that you didn't really mean but discreetly delivered to your mark.

She was tricky and artfully played us against one another. "Didn't Sophie look pretty, in spite of that awful balloon-shaped dress?" I knew perfectly well that if I agreed that Sophie looked pretty, my sister would hear I thought her dress was awful. I think Mother thought it was amusing, unaware that I grew up ill at ease, never quite sure who to trust and who to be afraid of.

Mother was desperate to get rid of me when I grew into an unattractive, unsavory teenager, and she campaigned to send me to boarding school. But her institutions of choice were anathema to me. So Mother struck a bargain with the Devil and packed me off to a hippie boarding school in Vermont. The school was a kind of naïve, experimental place where drugs were as available as toilet paper, and no one checked up on you. After a month or two, I went crazy and stayed in bed, until one morning I threw some clothes in my backpack and hitchhiked the 325 miles home.

New leaves shone green against the gray evening sky as I trudged up the hill toward our house. Tufts of grass sprouted between the bricks of the front walk, all so sweet and familiar, I almost felt safe.

Because I hadn't obtained my parents' permission to leave, I'd cooked up a flimsy cover story about the school letting me go home for a surprise visit. I couldn't have looked too healthy, since I'd been crying for hours, and I had stood on the edge of the highway screaming as loud as I could between rides. Plus, I'd gained about thirty pounds.

I vividly remember Mom coming to the door in a black turtleneck and a salmon-colored skirt. The Chinese bead necklace I'd coveted since I was old enough to want anything was around her neck. I was a horrid teenager, a person my mother was not equipped to deal with. I often hurt, humiliated, and frustrated her to no end. But I can't forget how she looked out through the screen and said, "Yes?" as though I were a stranger. I went absolutely hollow.

If I'd thought I might be welcome, I was mistaken. Mom kept me standing on the steps. She said through the screen that she had company, and they were just sitting down for dinner. "You have to understand that now you are a guest. You come home when you have an invitation," she said. But it dawned on her that she could not really send me away, and she let me in.

I watched TV in the study until the guests departed. But even then, when Mom called me to task, I was too undone to comment on my own condition. I slept in my old room, which seemed smaller than I remembered. The street light flickering through the leaves made a pattern on the wall like an old forgotten friend. I wept, unable to sleep because of a grief I could not name.

The panic oozing out of me was invisible to my parents, who hoped that if they ignored whatever had made me show up at home, it might just go away. Mom drove me to the bus stop and sent me back to school, where I went back to bed and flunked algebra and chemistry as a result. This time the school sent me home, and Mother was encumbered with me once again. She dedicated the next year to making sure I got through my final year of high school.

Ages later, when I was a parent trying to do my best and often failing, I began to feel sorry for all the hassle I'd caused Mom, never once considering life from her point of view. This was very noble of me, I thought, all things considered. I was also getting paranoid about what my own children would feel in years to come, when they were the ones pushing *my* wheelchair. So I started scripting an apology to her, which I rehearsed for years.

Walter was on the scene, but they had not yet married, so Mother was still gallivanting around without him. The opportunity to apologize came when Mother roped me into one of her harebrained schemes. She wanted to attend the Gathering of the Nations tribal dancing in Gallup, New Mexico. None of my brothers or sisters were willing to get suckered into this one, so I ended up driving Mother from Albuquerque to Gallup in a rented Cadillac.

Well, it turned out Mom had never bothered to check the dates, certain that the event she'd witnessed in 1936 would be at the same time, same place in 1997. The dances had ended the week before. Everyone was packed up and gone. So I turned the Cadillac around and drove back across the same splendid, empty landscape. In the passenger seat next to me, Mom's profile, suggestive of the American eagle and just as forbidding, was outlined against the desert. This was my moment.

"Mom, I am so sorry for all the hurt and aggravation I put you through," I said. At last, Mother and I would reconcile! No more dragging around that old bag of guilty bones. I waited, but after a few minutes, she still hadn't said anything. Maybe she didn't know it was her turn to apologize to *me*—for tying me to my bed, for sending Frances to school plays and teacher meetings (in her place), for all the items in *my* resentment inventory. "It must have been just awful," I said, prodding her. But Mom, over on her side of the Cadillac, said not a word, as though she might not have heard me. "How did you ever manage to forgive me?" I said loudly, shamelessly goading her. "For all those rude, ghastly, mean things—"

"Darling," she said, giving me a very gracious nod, "you don't even have to mention it."

I waited for her to say more, but she didn't. And she had heard me, all right. As I drove down the empty highway, I slowly understood that she had no gift-wrapped apology for me. On the contrary, she probably felt she'd put up with a lot, had done the best she could, and was now vindicated by my saying how sorry I was. Out of the corner of my eye, I could see the old American eagle, proud as ever, looking very pleased.

I had not foreseen this surprise ending, and I would have taken my apology back, if I could have. That smiling, silent profile was not what I'd bargained for. But I guess there is no such thing as a bargain when it comes to family.

One morning when I arrived for my monthly shift, Mom scuttled toward me, rolling her walker. She was wearing red pants and a white blouse, with a bright-yellow cardigan. Her shoes had been recently cleaned, and that white stuff around her feet was baby powder, which was a relief. Murbeth took good care of her, even if she was dressed like a kindergartner.

Mother's blank and dull face lit up like a sunflower. "Meggo, dear!" she said, with a huge toothy smile, lurching at me, hugging me, and ramming me with the walker. She was so glad to see me, pressing her face into my shoulder, gripping my arms. To share a moment of simple uncalculated love, my mother had had to become a dependent old lady with a dismantled intellect. I managed to disentangle myself and hang up my wet raincoat. The house was a tomb in rainy weather, dark and damp, which wasn't helping Mom's sad mood. "Walter is out," she said as we headed for the couch.

"He out with Cathy in the limo," Murbeth said. "To New York."

"They left for a good time," added Mom. Cathy often took her father out, leaving Mom at home. Mother resented this. It didn't bother me because I got to have her to myself. But with her somewhat Victorian social sensibility, a man's company was always worth more than any woman's. The real point was that Cathy had won the competition for today.

We settled into our accustomed spots, Mom reclining with her feet on the couch, me facing her in the wing chair, with my feet next to hers in a kind of girl-talk setup. Murbeth brought Mom a glass of cranberry juice with a straw. To make these séances more amenable, I had gotten into the habit of getting a decent latte on my way to the house. The only thing missing was a little light, because of those complicated timers.

I tried to think up lines of conversation that Mom could handle. Today, in the gloom, she was silent, depressed about Cathy and Walter. I'd never heard anything about her honeymoon aboard the *Queen Mary,* though I'd seen pictures of her wearing a very odd pleated cape, arm in arm with Dad, who was grinning. I brought up what I thought would be a happy reminiscence. "Oh, yes," Mom said with a sigh. "That's when your father told me I could not keep my job."

"You wanted to keep working?" I had never heard this angle before.

Mom's face flooded with regret. "Well, they'd told me I showed promise at Scribner's, you know. 'But the children come first,' he said. Hard words for a new bride to hear."

I suddenly saw Mom in a new light, one that illuminated the background. She gave up her job and her independence for Dad, whose priorities were his children, his job, and then his wife. So she had marked time. She'd gotten rid of all of us as quickly as she could, so she could finally have Dad to herself. But by the time we were all finally out of the house, it was too late. Dad had become an old man, too worn out to be an enthusiastic soul mate for his much younger wife, and perhaps unaware of her longings.

Poor Mom! Then her husband died. So she got a new husband, and what happened? She had to compete with Cathy! She had never been good at sharing. "Oh, Mom, how sad for you, and how hard," I said. And her old face revealed her surprise that this secret pain was understood—ironically, by one of her children.

Those hours on the couch were physically exhausting. My rear end was numb and my back hurt. But, really, when you get old that's about all you do. You sit. You might sit in different places, but once the legs go, you sit. I figured I might as well practice, so I'd be good and ready when my time came. With all this sitting around, old people will eventually tell you about their mothers and fathers. My mother was no exception.

My mother's father died before I was born and I barely remember my grandmother, so anything Mom said about them was interesting. Her father, Roland van Zeld, was a porter for the Indiana railroad when he met my grandmother Sophia Neuson. Her parents weren't too keen on this romantic attachment. Hoping to put an end to it, they sent Sophie to New York, where she studied light operetta.

Roland took penmanship lessons and wrote her letters in an elegant script to win her heart. They married. Eventually he became a successful stockbroker and moved his family to Oldhill. They had two daughters. The elder, Sally, died of appendicitis. As Christian Scientists, my grandparents wouldn't consent to an operation. Her death left them with one six-year-old daughter, Mabel. According to Mom, they weren't planning to have more children.

"Mother buried Sally and was just beginning to get back to herself, to be a person in her own right, to have friends and give parties—but then she and Daddy got stuck with me," she said.

You believe this kind of thing because someone *made* you feel that way. No child sees herself as a burden to her parents without some coaching, a hint dropped here and there, sometimes camouflaged by a good-natured smile.

Roland moved out of the marital bed and into the little narrow room adjacent to it. Mom became her father's best friend, reading books and listening to the radio with him while her mother went to Atlantic City by herself. "It was my fault," Mom told me. That's another conclusion you don't come up with on your own. I can just picture my grandmother getting fed up and justifying those departures with a few poisonous barbs on her way out the door. Where Mom's remaining sister was through all this, I don't know.

They lived in a fancy house with a sunken living room, vases in dramatic niches, and stars painted on the ceiling. I also learned that her family employed a butler named Walter. (Perhaps that accounted for Walter's secret appeal.)

When Mom was twelve she had attained her adult height of five feet, eight inches, which made her a social liability as far as her mother was concerned. "Poor Mama, saddled with such an unattractive, horsey child," Mom said. Eager to stunt this embarrassing growth, Grandmother made Mom smoke Camels and drink black coffee. I'll bet her mother did some other weird things, too—all for her own good. And I'll bet that's why Addie couldn't bear it when I committed the crime of gaining weight—thus becoming "unattractive." In this scenario, I was cast as the inadequate, disappointing daughter that she, the Mom in the script, had to resent. No wonder Addie hadn't apologized that time in New Mexico. She'd have had to forgive herself, the awkward, galling girl whom she was determined to punish. Addie was so smart, it was hard to believe that the key to her crazy parenting was, perhaps, so simple.

Now the lights really went on, and I was not spared from the glare. What was I doing, all grown up, *my* children a thousand miles away with a babysitter, while I struggled to win Addie's approval? I had allowed myself to become her surrogate, carrying her unrequited love.

As I sat on the couch, the lily petals fell onto the coffee table until the stems were bare, and Mom slowly brought forth the grief and self-hatred she'd carried from childhood into old age. But the eyes that looked out of her old face were still searching for the approval of her mother, long gone.

"Who said you weren't beautiful?" I asked. "Who said you caused those problems? Your parents were the grown-ups; you were a child and they were jerks. They were lucky to have had you!" Mom didn't respond. "You didn't do anything wrong!" I realized how angry I was at my dead grandparents—I was practically shouting.

"I miss them so," Mom said. "Mama and dear Papa."

Well, I was surprised, but I shouldn't have been. You can't reconcile the people you love with the things they do, especially to you. You are stuck with loving them. Who knows what subterranean hurts drove my grandmother off to Atlantic City? Perhaps, though people do awful things to one another, there's no one to pin the blame on in the end.

Mom rolled her head, tilting her eyes toward the window and the fenced yard beyond. "Is that some kind of a dog?" she asked me, raising her bony finger to point. "Some kind of deer?" My heart sank. Her sudden trips to Kooky Town were always disturbing. I never knew where we were going to end up.

I got up to look, scrambling for what I'd say when there was nothing there. But in a corner of the yard, a large gray doe was cropping the grass close to the post where the lawn mower didn't reach. She was big and wild and unexpected and glorious. Both Mom and I caught our breath. For a moment she looked right at us (though more than likely she glimpsed her own reflection in the window). Then, with a flick of her tail, she gathered herself and soared effortlessly, weightlessly over the railing, leaving us wildly, wildy happy.

One summer, the year Dad retired, Mother and Dad and I went to a resort in Maine—just me with the two of them. The path from our cottage to the main lodge wound through a grove of white pine and bushes of black and red raspberries that glittered in the early-morning dew. Spiderwebs sparkled like rigging. And every blade of grass, every leaf and branch, was transformed by morning mist into a magical world. Fiddleheads unfurled themselves toward the light high above. And when the wind blew, last year's pinecones, the ones that held on all winter, fell at last with a thud.

Winding its way through the dark trunks, the path suddenly broke onto the open beach and white Maine sun shining thinly on flat pebbles. The cold, clear sea rose and fell until it met the sky in a thin line, far away. Starfish slid along the bottom, catching dark-blue mussels in their arms. Barnacles grew on the rock cliffs, and in tidal pools concealed by golden-brown seaweed, periwinkles convened, their spires shining in the sun like tiny cathedrals.

Mother and I left Dad on the beach while we scrabbled together over the broad backs of glacial rocks, finding the tide pools brimming with mysteries. We didn't talk as we hopped from wonder to wonder.

The swell of waves sucking the pebbles down the beach, then spraying them back again, sounded almost like breathing. I can see Mom's face, freckled and smooth, her eyes blue, her brown hair blown all over the place. Grinning, full of appetite, and happy—this is the mother I saw for a moment when the deer jumped over the fence.

Chapter Seven

TO HER HEALTH

Compared with the venerable Bank of Oldhill, the bank I use today resembles a self-service gas station. Back then—dwarfed by vaulted ceilings, giant chandeliers, and acres of marble—my childhood self clutched my mother's hand and whispered so as not to disturb the balding, three-piece-suited bankers at their desks, on our way to a line of deferential tellers. The dollar was worthy of respect if not veneration, and I'll bet that sleeping on a mattress full of cash had to be a spiritual experience for those who believed.

Much has changed in the banking industry. The starchy Old Boys promulgating fiduciary sobriety have been replaced by casual youngsters with Blackberry devices, and the nice tellers by whirring cash machines.

Mother never did learn to use a cash machine—thank God—nor did she wish to. The only civilized way to obtain cash was from a teller. Besides, the real point now was to say hello, to be treated like a regular human being. She didn't need the money, but each week Mom withdrew $160 (possibly the amount of some vestigial household salary).

Walter, of course, insisted on going with her, which meant that Jeffrey and Murbeth had to go along, too, while Cassandra drove the car. Thus, a routine weekly errand became a mounted expedition.

In preparation, Walter and Mother cloistered themselves in Mom's office to write the check, an operation that required the two of them. Mom dictated and Walter wrote in the dates and the amounts. Then Mom, aiming her pen at the line, made the chicken scratches that passed for her signature. In bygone days, she must have felt very powerful visiting the bank, withdrawing the money, counting it into envelopes, and judiciously handing out wages. Now the ritual trip to the bank helped revive her former sense of potency.

On this particular day, Mother and Walter advanced on the teller and presented the check. "I'd like that in ones," said Mom, who enjoyed the feel of a big wad of cash swelling her wallet. The teller, who was new, stared at the check and shook her head.

"You are sure you want it in ones?"

"I do," Mom said. "I prefer ones."

The teller frowned. "Do you mind if I count it in back and bring it out?"

"That will be splendid," Mother said.

Mother and Walter ended up with two grocery bags stuffed with greenbacks, because Walter made the check out for $1,600, not $160. And on the way home in the car, he broke one of the bags.

I know all this because Cassandra called me.

"They look like they making a salad back there. Jeffrey and Murbeth grabbing at the money, Walter yelling, and this green stuff flying around." Cassandra couldn't stop laughing. One-dollar bills were whirling into the air, out the car windows, and onto the sidewalks, where passersby could not believe their luck. "One man pulling money off a bush!" Cassandra reported. She parked the car and recovered what money she could. When she finally got it all counted, and the stacks lined up on the kitchen counter, a few hundred dollars were missing, just more damning evidence of the financial mayhem in Departure Lounge.

Money was running out of the house through every available aperture, including the mail slot. Walter had a love-hate relationship with the U.S. Postal Service. On the one hand, the mail was something to look forward to each day; you just never knew what was going to arrive. That was the love part. The hate part was the sense of inadequacy those envelopes brought him. On the whole I'd say they canceled each other out, and the Departure Lounge would have been better off without mail altogether.

Every day but Sunday, when God and the post office took a break, the mailman climbed the awkward flagstone steps between 11 A.M. and 2 P.M. Walter lurked around the front door, peering out, checking his watch, and sometimes running his hand through the mail slot, to be sure his eyes weren't deceiving him.

Once the avalanche of mail came, the gargantuan task of sorting it began. It was an insidious kind of home invasion, because Walter was on the World's Biggest Suckers list, and the direct mail he got shamelessly manipulated his vanity and fear to get at his wallet.

The people who design junk mail are the same guys who design stock certificates. Phony seals and official-looking stamps were all over these things, making them look as bona fide as money itself and as official as the federal government. Even Express Mail came to the door requiring a signature. With its silver envelope and TOP PRIORITY COURIER SERVICE and URGENT stamped all over it, who wouldn't get excited?

Walter believed that any letter that began, "Dear Walter," had to be from someone he knew. Convinced that he must know them from someplace he just couldn't recall, he sent money to both Linda Tripp and Monica Lewinsky, who apparently still needed money to pay off their legal fees. "Those poor girls," Walter said. "They say they need my help right away." He thought about it for a minute. "I think that's rude," he added. "I don't feel they should be rushing me."

He also had a lot of sympathy for Oliver North, who, on behalf of some right-wing organization, told him, "We are counting on you, Walter, to make the difference."

The sweepstakes racketeers considerately communicated with Walter in large-face type for easier reading, and engaged him in all the busywork of a tax return, with columns, lists, and exacting instructions. The whole package was geared to exploit Walter's self-importance, while counting on his confusion to cover up the nonsense involved. Afraid of failing to handle the documents properly, he sat for hours reading and rereading this junk, underlining certain phrases and dates in different colored pens, and muttering to himself.

Each solicitation was legitimized in Walter's mind by various gimmicks and procedures. "Affix the qualifying code to line one. Scratch off the Gold Seal to reveal your personal bonus code. Affix your personal bonus code to your entry card. Fill out your check and record your qualifying code on the right-hand corner. Then place the entry card in the self-enclosed envelope with your check . . ." Walter wrote quite a few checks.

Walter regarded sweepstakes as investment deals and tried to keep track of the various forms and submission requirements, in order to maintain his eligibility in scam after scam. He detailed his "investments" in a special notebook, recording the potential return and notification dates.

The real trouble came when Walter put three thousand dollars on his credit card, in response to a crook who had the audacity to call him repeatedly on the phone. William listened in on one conversation, during which the guy tried to get Walter to look for his wallet: "Is it in your pocket, or maybe on your nightstand? No? How about under the bed?"

Walter tried to convince Mother that one particular sweepstakes was a once-in-a-lifetime opportunity, and as he was a little short, that she needed to get involved in this fantastic investment. "You have to be willing to take a risk now and again, if you want to get anywhere," he said—which, by the way, was his philosophy on running red lights.

"If we can get the money to them ASAP, we can have seven hundred and forty-eight thousand dollars by next Tuesday!" Walter said. He wheedled, pestered, and bullied until she said, "Fine!" and five grand sprouted wings and flew away.

Walter was devastated each time he didn't win, and Cathy was not too pleased, either. "I can hardly get him to sign the checks to pay Jeffrey," she complained. (Walter maintained he could manage fine on his own, and he resented spending money for services he felt he didn't need.)

The staff took to hiding the mail until Luanne could go through it, leaving only the tamest correspondence for Walter's perusal. Outgoing mail also had to be screened, to make sure he hadn't managed to get his hands on a checkbook.

Of course, Mom and Walter were entitled to spend their money as they liked, because they were both legally competent. Competency is complex and so hard to contest that several lawyers cautioned me away from it, advising that even if we won, we'd ruin our relationship with our mother, and things weren't quite bad enough to warrant it. But I'm telling you, any judge who spent a weekend at the Departure Lounge would hand over guardianship of both of them to anyone who could walk and chew gum at the same time.

Until that day, though, as long as Walter and Mother could sign checks, people would find ways to get their money.

Mom and Walter sat day after day on the same couches and chairs, until the upholstery became like unwashed clothing. The TV room, site of many spills and catastrophic incidents, was particularly disturbing.

After dinner, Mom and Walter spent their evenings in this room, planted in front of the TV, which was inevitably roaring at full volume. (Walter would have happily spent his days there, too.) Mother was stationed in the loveseat across from the enormous TV, while Walter manned the remote from the rocker. The original room decor sported white cushions with blue piping. The carpet over the fake slate floor was also white, risky in any household. When it was new it had seemed a bit sterile.

Well, that wasn't a problem anymore. The upholstery provided a fertile breeding ground for who knows what kind of pathogens. You really didn't want to sit on the little couch, which advertised Mom's incontinence problem. And I'd rather die than get near the greenish dark oil stains on the back of Walter's chair. So I was relieved to learn that Mom wanted to redecorate.

Sometime after the great cash debacle, Mom, aided by Murbeth, Walter, Jeffrey, and Cassandra, wobbled into a small decorating shop down the street from the bank. An appointment was made for a home visit from the proprietress, who arrived punctually with several books of fabric samples. The lady was a bit disheveled but very nice, and she took the trouble to sit and have a cup of tea with Mom and Walter, something very few people were willing to do. The nice lady came back a few more times with a measuring tape and wallpaper samples—and left with a check for $25,000, the deposit.

Mom described her plans, which I couldn't quite visualize with the same enthusiasm. "There will be holly flowers and bumblebees, with a thing that rolls like a footstool for coffee! All fresh!" She didn't mention the check.

Decorating was not Mom's forte. What she called "orange" I would call "brown." Colors that should have been harmonious, by her description, were not. She once redecorated our comfy old playroom to resemble a Holiday Inn reception area, complete with industrial carpeting. Still, anything would be better than that unsanitary TV room.

Mother was fully animated with the happy prospect of home improvements, but the nice lady did not reappear for the next appointment. When called, the shop's phone clicked over to an answering machine. Luanne discovered Mom's check had been cashed. (The nice bank manager who'd volunteered to watchdog Mom's account for just such transactions had since been transferred. I wished she'd called to let me know.) Luanne hopped in her car and drove over to the store, because $25,000 is a lot of money.

The display window was empty, except for one bolt of dusty fabric and some crumpled paper cups. The door was locked, and a small notice in the window indicated that the business was closed. With more sleuthing, Luanne discovered that shortly after her visit with Mother, the nice lady had had a nervous breakdown and was currently in a mental hospital. Mom's money was gone. Zip, zero. Bankruptcy had been filed.

Mother was upset. Not only had she lost the money, but the nice lady wouldn't be visiting again—*and* she wouldn't be getting rid of her smelly upholstery. "Presumably, she had a happy time with my check," Mom said, "but my surrounds are quite bad, bad, and bad. With my lady locked up, how will I continue?"

Along with the money, Mom was robbed of the pleasure of being an important client with a serious plan.

Again the trusty Yellow Pages came through and, after we had carefully checked their references, the Classic Chintz decorating company was scheduled for a visit. Once again Mom had a great time picking out fabric and wallpaper over the teapot. Everybody was very happy.

Then I got a phone call from the new nice lady. "I'm so sorry to be a bother, but it seems your mother gave us an invalid American Express card number." Mom often rattled off "from memory" series of numbers that might or might not relate to her account.

"We can't start without it," she said. I did not want to hold up the project. For one thing, I was really looking forward to sitting on a nice, clean couch. Rather than making the necessary barrage of calls between Halifax and Oldhill, I covered the purchase myself. I could handle a couple of hundred dollars for some piping.

But nothing is ever simple. To make a long story short, my account number was put on Mom's file and the whole project wound up on my credit card, which, incidentally, I share with my husband. And soon enough, Rob was standing at an Avis counter in a faraway city, late for a business meeting and not happy when his card was declined because of Mom's new upholstery.

When I tried to explain the whole thing to Mother so she could pay me back and bail out my marriage, she said, "No, no, dear. Your sister paid for that and I've already sent her a check." No good deed, no matter how small, goes unpunished. Not one.

Sophie laughed when I told her this story. "I knew that check was too good to be true!" she said, and she sent me the money.

In retrospect, many decisions we made concerning Mom's money and valuables look feckless. But at the time, we were forced to choose between bad options, and fast.

Mom had an embarrassingly large jewelry box, more of a small bureau, really, with a bunch of drawers. Dad had given my mother rings and pins to commemorate the arrival of us children, for anniversaries, and sometimes just for plain old romance. A hoard of Italian gold chains filled one drawer. Another contained a substantial collection of rings: a sapphire, a ruby, and others nested in diamonds, the kind of artless, clunky stuff worn by dowagers in novels, impressive for sheer size.

Mom had also bought herself strings of jade, coral, and lapis beads, pearls, and a bunch of turquoise from her Navajo phase. The more costumey pieces—semiprecious necklaces, fake pearls for traveling, gold-plated pendants with cat's eyes and glass—had their own drawer. When I was little, it all looked to me like magic treasure.

After Dad's death, *I* gave Mom jewelry, reasoning that someone should. Most of the stuff I could afford was fake, except for one extravagant topaz-and-diamond ring. Right after Dad died, a local jeweler told me Dad had planned to give it to Mom. I fell for it, of course, and my sister and I scrambled for the money, which was considerable. Mother made a point of wearing the ring when we were around, but I never got the feeling she liked it.

When Mom came home after her stroke, she often asked for her jewelry box, much the way she'd once demanded her purse. "Ring, rings, rings and things!" she crowed. Fondling the treasure trove was a reassuring and pleasing activity when few things were much fun.

There comes a time when the sentimental value of family heirlooms is blotted out by the money they're worth—usually from the heir's point of view, of course. Mother's jewelry was a valuable, not to mention vulnerable, asset. But it was worth something to her only if she could get her hands on it. From a money perspective, we should have locked it in a vault. But then Mother would no longer be able to enjoy it, which seemed like prematurely consigning her to the glue factory. So William and I compromised, stashing the jewelry box in a locked closet and hiding the key.

In the early days of the Departure Lounge, at Mom's request, I lugged out the treasure and, under the spell of shiny things, we played a weird version of dress-up. Mom was resplendent in four pearl necklaces, six or seven brooches, rings, pins, and some earrings. I put on whatever was left. And then we sang, among other selections, "There Is Nothing Like a Dame," from *South Pacific,* which made us positively giddy.

Then one day I opened the box and the rings were gone. Without saying anything, I checked the rest of the collection. All the gold chains were gone, and many of the pins and brooches. Only the costume jewelry and small pieces remained. I couldn't believe all that serious hardware, easily $100,000 worth, had walked out the door.

Plenty of temps I never laid eyes on had been through the house, substituting for our regulars, who sometimes couldn't make a shift. An observant four-year-old could have figured out how to get into the jewelry box. Or maybe one of the old gang had copied a key, slipped in when the house was vacant on a Sunday, and had fun parading around in Mom's gold chains. Naturally, I preferred to imagine that an actual robber was to blame.

I had no one but myself to blame—and, of course, William. I could blame him, too, and that was a relief. Maybe we should have ignored Addie's feelings and put the stuff in the bank.

Alice and I arranged to check the contents of the jewelry box against the insurance inventory. And we ended up going over it with Mother, though I'd schemed to leave her out of this unhappy affair.

The three of us gathered in Mom's office. After going though the charade of getting the empty jewelry box out of our "secure" locked closet, I said, "It seems like some of your rings are missing." Mom slowly turned her head toward me and asked in a monotone, as though expecting this, "The blue one? The red ruby, too? The topaz from you girls?" Her face was as blank as a sheet of rain, as I detailed the missing items.

"We could try to collect on the insurance," said Alice, sitting rather forlornly with the useless inventory.

"Then the police will come," Mom said. The police and insurance people would, indeed, come, and they'd grill everyone in the house.

Resignation settled over Mom's features, not anger or outrage, but surrender. "I don't want to live that way," she said, "everyone watching each other."

"Mother, we should find out who did this." *I* was outraged. *I* felt taken advantage of, too, not to mention the money involved.

Although so distressed her lips trembled, Mom shook her head. To her, the loss of her jewelry was just one more loss in the context of many, one more step into humiliation and despair. "I don't want to know," she said. She didn't want to know that the trusted person who washed her in the shower, dressed her, helped her though her day, and put her to bed at night might think so little of her.

Mom sniffed, licked her lips, and without any change of expression, had an accident all over the couch, graphically summing up the whole situation.

Alice was horrified. I'd had worse moments with Mom's bodily functions. "Get a couple of towels," I told Alice, giving her a chance to escape as I snapped on rubber gloves. I turned to Mom, ready with the cheerful bravado that gets you through humiliation, but she had checked out. Gone to a faraway place where she'd find her jewelry right there in the box where it was supposed to be. She'd left this useless rag doll behind to be disrobed, disinfected, and redressed.

The staff knew what the jewelry was worth, and they knew we weren't seriously doing anything to find out who had made off with it. Just one of those rings would be a fortune for anyone working there. Our cavalier lack of effort had to be a slap in the face. After all, if we could afford to kiss that jewelry good-bye, we could afford to pay them more than the pittance they were getting.

Immediately, Murbeth threatened to quit if we didn't pay her an extra $350 per week in cash. "You know you paying me nothing," she said. I didn't want to lose Murbeth. Mom liked her well enough, and replacing her would be a nightmare. "I'm trying to bring my son here," she told me. "He not doing well in Jamaica." Then she told me she also worked a weekend job at a nursing home. William, Alice, and I saw her point.

Of course, then everyone else knew we upped the ante for Murbeth, and pretty soon Jeffrey was dropping some not-so-subtle hints.

"A little more money around *my* house sure would come in handy," he said.

Needing guidance, I called on Marilyn, the agency supervisor, who set me straight. "While the staff is prohibited from soliciting money from clients," said Marilyn, shifting in her seat, "you should feel free to express your appreciation from time to time."

"Am I supposed to be tipping people?"

"Of course you aren't obliged to," she said—but clearly, a decent person would. William and I should have been tipping our staff all along. The money flying out of the car, the upholstery mess, now the jewelry—our sheer carelessness with money was an insult to their sacrifice and struggle.

So now we tipped all the time. I hugged Murbeth and Jeffrey the minute I walked in the door, even if they didn't care about me one bit—the boss lady with the big wallet—and I handed out envelopes all around to get it over with. Then Jeffrey wouldn't have to act like my friend unless he felt like it.

I really hate the part of life where the truth of love and the reality of money collide.

Mom cooked up a scheme to repatriate her jewelry box. "I will procure a large, large ring," she announced to Cassandra. "And fine paintings of art." My parents had collected a few very nice paintings, the kind that said sophistication and good taste. The whole experience of collecting was gratifying, and not everyone knew how to do it. Addie was out to prove she could still exercise her discerning sensibilities.

And so Mother—sans Walter, who had a doctor's appointment—embarked in the Buick with Cassandra and Murbeth as her entourage. Jeffrey came along to mind the car, because parking it was not going to be an option. First stop, the Greystone Gallery on Fifth Avenue. Behind the elegant stone facade and heavy glass doors, art and money changed hands in the deliberate, discreet quiet that descended the instant those doors clicked shut. At the Greystone, they didn't even play Muzak.

Ill at ease in the gallery's "members only" atmosphere, Cassandra fended off her discomfort by staring at the floor while Murbeth took the opposite tack, sniffing with disdain and rolling her eyes. But for Mother, it was like coming home. Attired in her olive-green St. John knit suit and foot-pinching Pappagallos, she settled into the faux Louis XIV chair with relief. Reflected in the gallery manager's deferential manner, she glimpsed the discerning, intelligent woman she so missed at home.

An unethical establishment might have taken this opportunity to unload a couple of turkeys on a blind old lady. Cassandra called me in a panic. "Your mom putting a hundred and twenty thousand dollars on her credit card! They say they deliver next week, but she walking out with nothing!" I barely reassured her. And with nothing but a slender receipt, the three ladies laboriously crammed back into the car for the one-block drive down Fifth Avenue to Tiffany and the replacement of rings.

But, far from the white-gloved domain she remembered, the aisles at Tiffany's were crowded with noisy shoppers in sweatpants, gawking at price tags and yelling into cell phones. According to Cassandra (who called me *again*), Mom circumambulated a few display cases, then pointedly stopped, flourished her hand, and sniffed, "I've always considered Tiffany garish and vulgar. Onward to Cartier!" Although incapable of turning on her heel, encumbered as she was with a helper on each side, she managed to wheel the three of them into a pretty snappy 180-degree turn, and they marched out the door.

Jeffrey was roused from another little car nap, and once again Cassandra and Murbeth loaded Mom into the car to travel five blocks down Fifth. Leaving Jeffrey to shepherd the car, they descended on the smaller and less frenzied Cartier. This proved more to Mother's satisfaction, although Cassandra's comfort level plummeted. She might not know anything about paintings, but she had met plenty of crooks who tried to sell her jewelry. Just because the man behind the case wore a suit didn't mean he wasn't a swindler.

While Mom fondled one diamond ring after another, her arthritic knuckles preventing her from trying them on, Cassandra eyeballed the price tags. The higher the price, the more nervous she got. Finally, Cassandra could stand it no longer.

"We have to get home, Miss Addie, because Walter's waiting for you," she lied. "We come back tomorrow and pick the biggest one."

"Mother getting tired after all this excitement," Murbeth chimed in, sick of standing around, fanning herself with her magazine.

While Murbeth yanked Mom to her feet, Cassandra neutralized the salesman by asking for his business card. "We'll call you," she said. And, whatever Mom's objections, they whisked her away.

"I seen bigger diamonds that don't cost five hundred dollars, and him asking thirty, forty thousand, knowing Addie blind!" Cassandra later reported, proud of herself for protecting her charge. And while I was eternally grateful for her concern, I felt bad for Mom; her happy plan had been spoiled, and she had been reduced in the eyes of her salesman-prince.

And why shouldn't she buy herself diamonds if she wanted to? Of course, given the fate of the last batch, she might have been better off with substitutes—not rocks from Cartier, but cubic zirconium from Kmart.

However, I was able to arrange a couple of successful substitutions in Mom's life that cheered her up and lifted her spirits more than a whole bunch of big new diamonds might have. (I was incredibly proud of myself.)

One of the problems of old age is that your friends die off. And if they aren't dead, they're in the same shape you are and have a hard time staying in touch because, like Mom, they can't dial the phone. The few mobile friends Mom *did* have left were unwilling to witness the fate *they* held at bay by clutching the unraveling hem of their own independence. Mom was increasingly lonely and blue, descending into a deep, mournful, and resentful sadness.

The real curse of old age is not the looming grave; it's outliving your friends.

When Mom ventured out to the supermarket or to get her hair

done, no one recognized her. Even the reliable faces at the bank had been replaced with new people who didn't know the iconic Addie Henry. Her reputation no longer preceded her. Instead, Mrs.—what was her name? Huber?—and that scary husband of hers were a trial and a cross.

Each time I said good-bye, Mom begged me not to leave her alone in this alien place. Sick with guilt, I'd pry her fingers from mine. But even if I *had* uprooted my family and moved next door, I couldn't bring back the people she knew and the faces she loved, especially not her own, now a wrinkled stranger who humiliated her. Cathy got Walter out a few times a week; we needed to get Mom in touch with more people, even if we had to pay them.

Cassandra took "in touch" literally. "That lady needs a massage," she said. Now that Walter was prodded into wakefulness during the day and was sleeping in his own bed at night, professional bathing and dressing was about all the physical contact Mom got. Babies who aren't caressed fail to thrive; maybe adults suffer similarly. Mom hated her body, this clumsy, broken-down thing she dragged around every day. She sat down almost all the time now, with only tiny walks to the table or bathroom. Maybe her spirit was withering from inactivity and from being ignored.

So, thanks to Cassandra, Felicia came into our lives late that summer. Felicia was a massage therapist and a firefighter for the Oldhill Fire Department. Twice a week, she arrived at Mom's front door in white scrubs, bringing her massage table and a jumbo-size serving of spirituality along with her. With her long blond hair and Birkenstocks, Felicia had the physical presence of a farm girl used to handling men and animals. In fact, she could confidently handle anyone—if need be, simply throw them over her shoulder. She may have been full of angel talk, but Felicia was anything but flighty.

Mom wasn't too thrilled with the prospect, but Felicia got her naked and up on the table in no time, by letting her know there was no other option. Just the way you get a horse to accept a saddle.

"Come on now, Miss Adelaide. Let's just find out where all this negativity you're putting out is coming from. There's an angel in your heart, and she's telling me that you're mighty sad in there." This is just the kind of gooey talk that made my mother throw up, but Felicia was irresistible. With blunt goodwill and a lot of muscle, she had Mom cornered. Literally. Cassandra helped Mom disrobe, and I helped Felicia drape her with sheets and wrap warm towels around her feet.

Mom's old body was like an artifact no longer in use. When she was younger, she exuded a kind of sweaty healthiness, the kind of physicality that goes with tennis rather than sex appeal. But now her body was beyond sexuality, beyond appetite. Pearly white and practically transparent, the ropy skin draped her bones like a casing that might soon slough off.

Under Felicia's touch, Mom sighed and moaned with relief, and after an hour, fell asleep on the massage table. She was a little embarrassed about this massage business, afraid I might think it was motivated by vanity. "I am not concerned about my figure, you know," she said, looking down and patting her bony hips. "The massaging is not for my shape. I am not trying to lose weight but to build myself up."

In any case, Felicia won her over. Mom became a real enthusiast and wanted to push old Walter into getting a massage, too. "I think it would be so good for him," she confided.

Perhaps due to his dementia, Walter couldn't keep track of his physical position. He stood at an alarming forward tilt. When seated, he assumed spectacular gravity-defying positions. Sometimes he'd lean forward, with his elbows planted on the chair seat, his feet on the floor, and his bottom suspended in the air, poised to do a somersault.

But I never saw him fall. Contrary to his frail appearance, Walter could hold these poses, teetering back and forth, for hours. Every night after dinner, when we watched *Wheel of Fortune* (without which the day was not complete), Mother and I sat cozily on the loveseat while Walter dangled from his chair, oblivious to his bizarre contortions.

When Felicia rang the doorbell, Mom prodded Walter. "Come on along now, dearie. Felicia is good at this massaging."

"Sure, Mr. Huber. I'd be happy to give you a nice rubdown," boomed Felicia with extra-strength heartiness.

Walter took one look at Felicia and her duffel bag of equipment, and shuffled backward out of the room.

"If I were doing athletics, football, perhaps, I might need such things. But I have no need at this time. Should I take up sports at some future time, I will let you know," he said, and escaped.

Her human friends weren't the only ones my mother missed. Until her stroke, I never saw Mom without a book at hand. Books were her most intimate companions. They had gotten her through everything in life, including a teenage bout of tuberculosis. Now, for the first time, books were no comfort. But even though she couldn't read, she often sat comforted by the familiar weight of a book propped open on her lap.

I read to her when I visited, but then I'd be gone for weeks at a time and neither of us could remember where the story had left off. Audiobooks weren't useful, because Mother's fugue-like mental state made it very hard to embrace a voice emanating from a machine. And the trusty Yellow Pages had no listing for "readers." Failing that, I hit on the idea that the library would have a list of community-minded book lovers, lining up to read aloud. They did not—nor did the high schools, even though students had to fulfill a community service requirement. The YMCA couldn't give me any leads, and Mom's minister was way too busy to read the Bible to an old lady. I started calling bookstores.

For years, Mom had patronized the Book Room. When Mom's eyesight failed, the owner, Wanda, carefully selected, wrapped, and mailed the Christmas and birthday books Mom bestowed. To my dismay, Wanda's Book Room was defunct. I started calling all the stores in the Yellow Pages, but no one had a quick solution or any real interest in my quest. Finally I called Oldhill Book Center, and Wanda answered the phone. She immediately agreed to read to Mom several mornings a week.

Mother now had a reason to use the good teapot, insist on fresh flowers, and see herself reflected in the mirror of Wanda's admiration and respect. They embarked on *The Empire of the Arabs,* by John Bagot Glubb, a subject no one else in the household could begin to discuss.

But Wanda offered my mother something better than books and a tea party. Wanda had real, hard-core problems. Nothing perked Mom up like an opportunity to give advice. In the intimacy that arose between them, Wanda revealed that her husband was dying, and the days left to him were long, exhausting, and sad for her. Setting her own despair aside, Mother offered Wanda respite, through her remarkable sympathy and understanding.

Mom really mattered to Wanda in the present tense, and for a while Wanda's misery brought Mom back to life. I frankly considered this bit of orchestration a victory, because most of the stuff I try to engineer for others' own good doesn't work out. But Wanda and Felicia couldn't show up every day. The contrast of their occasional companionship with Mom's more frequent loneliness made everyday life even harder to bear, and she continued to spiral downward.

In the early days of her incapacity, Mom's big project had been getting well. Motivated by that goal, she was willing to put up with a lot of bossing from me, William, Alice, Murbeth, Cassandra, and her doctors. She was willing to use the walker and to work hard in physical therapy. It's the only reason she complied at all with not drinking, at least at home. "When I am better" was the theme song around the house, and we were all singing it. None of us is immune to hope.

But the new eye doctor, the young stupid one, told Mom, "I'm sorry. Your eyes are not going to improve. In fact, they may get worse." And the neurologist said, "You have brain shrinkage, which is, of course, irreversible." Thanks to the experts, Mom's hope collapsed into despair. If she couldn't look forward to recovery, she didn't want to live.

When I was going to college in New York, Mom and I occasionally met at the University Club for lunch or tea. One day as we were cozily stationed on those nice yellow sofas in the ladies' sitting room, tea in hand, Mother cleared her throat and said, "Meg, I hope you are still smoking marijuana occasionally," as though encouraging me to go to the gym. Since I'd spent my teenage years red-eyed and smiling and praying not to get caught, this was a bit of a switch.

"Mother, don't be ridiculous," I said, denying and lying.

Mom went on. "Because if I ever get cancer and have to go on chemotherapy, I want to be sure you know how to buy the stuff for me."

"Mom, I don't even smoke cigarettes!"

She raised an eyebrow. "Well, if you really don't use marijuana yourself, I want you to get busy and meet some people who do, just in case I need the stuff." Mother continued in this happy vein of thought. "And if I get senile or Parkinson's or anything like that, will you please poison me or hold a pillow over my face?"

"Of course I will," I said glibly, agreeing to terms I never thought she or I would confront.

"Good," she said. "I'm counting on you. Now, dear, is it my imagination, or have you put on a few pounds?"

I choked on my tea. In Mother's book, matricide was nothing compared to getting fat. Instantly my self-respect fled, my body seemed to swell, and my clothes tightened around me. Damp half-moons spread under my armpits. At that moment I was perfectly willing to put a pillow over her head and smother her right in public. I can tell you only the absence of a pillow held me back.

Years later, when her friends were dying and the doctors seemed to be postponing death rather than restoring health, Mom asked me to renew this death contract. I had kids by then and I pulled out of the deal. "Mom, I can't go to jail until the children are out of college," I told her, trying to make a joke. But she looked a little panicky.

Mother didn't feel secure without an exit strategy, because she'd already looked long and hard at the prospect of a drawn-out death. When she was nineteen, tuberculosis almost killed her. After two years in bed, she finally turned the corner and began to recover, but she'd stockpiled sleeping pills under her mattress, just in case.

Now, as outlined by her doctors, a slow and continuous decline was all she had to look forward to. But now, when she needed them, she had no stash of pills to hasten the journey, and no one to turn to for help. Even if she'd had the physical strength and the mental fortitude to come up with a plan, she was never alone long enough to do herself in. The only thing she had the power to do was fall—and hope it would eventually kill her.

As documented in the staff log, Mom fell twenty-two times in one month. The instant Murbeth, Cassandra, or I retrieved her from the floor, she fell down again. "I am so hoping that myself will not get up," she told me with tears of frustration, "but even that I can't do."

Murbeth took the tough-love approach. "There is nothing happening to Mother that isn't happening to people all over the world. Plenty of people alone, sick, with nothing and no one. And you living in this nice home, and your children who come around," Murbeth said, hoisting Mom to her feet after a nosedive, which I had failed to prevent. "Now, now," Murbeth said, patting Mother when she started to cry. "Now then, wipe your face and have some tea with this daughter here. And smile for her so she come back."

The only thing I could come up with was antidepressants (which I could not believe no one else had thought of before). As I was sorting this out with her medical experts, I chanced to discover that Mom was taking a double dose of blood thinner, prescribed by two doctors who, despite my best efforts, had failed to speak to each other. About a thousand phone calls later, I got that straightened out, and eventually carted Mom off to a new doctor and returned with a jug of Zoloft.

Zoloft did relieve Mom's depression, but it didn't improve her outlook. Rather than cheering her up, it revived her determination to die. Infused with anger, she clomped around the house, hell-bent on thwarting any attempt to keep her upright and alive.

You'd be standing there, helping her out of a chair, heaving her onto her feet, and the instant you loosened your grip—splat—she collapsed. In a move that would make a stunt artist wince, she released her legs like a string puppet and hit the floor. She was bruised blue, yellow, and brown up and down her arms, legs, and frequently her forehead. You'd help her up, and down she'd go again.

Mom had a plan, and she was sticking to it. Trying to kill herself renewed her interest in living.

Marilyn, the agency supervisor, did her best, using the old third-party ploy to leverage some guilt. "Miss Addie, you are making it very hard for my staff to do their job, which is to keep you safe. How would you feel if your client did everything she could to make you fail?"

Normally, a dressing-down from Marilyn had some effect. But Mom looked away, refusing to accept this analysis. "Then let them work elsewhere!" Mom said, her rebellion fueled by newfound Zoloft fury.

William and I rigged up baby monitors in every room, so that Murbeth and Jeffrey could spy on her at all times. Of course, it drove them crazy, because they had to lug around the receivers, which hissed and crackled annoyingly. The household shuddered with turmoil. Everyone's nerves were frayed, except for Mom, who, between bouts of victory, went catatonic with despair. How much fun can it be spending all your mental energy planning your next fall?

Her strategy was having a bad effect on Walter. Every time Mom lowered her head, thrust her weight forward, and prepared to launch, Walter jumped up and roughly pushed her back into her seat, yelling, "Watch her! Watch her!" and setting off the baby monitors, which shrieked in every room. Mom glowered at him, ready to spit. Walter, his eyeballs on fire, yelled, "You stay in that chair, goddamn it!"

"I will not!" Mom yelled right back. "I shall wish to do as I want!" Mother looked, dare I say, rather pleased with herself at causing this ruckus.

It occurred to me more than once that a little clothesline might just do the trick, discreetly tying her to the chair, a tactic she had not hesitated to use on me. The urge to tie her up was hard to resist.

Finally Marilyn folded up the walker, stuck it in the closet, and extracted the wheelchair from the car, where it was kept for excursions. The beat-up, black leather thing was rolled over to Mother with a formality and deliberateness impossible to ignore. "Mrs. Huber, the staff is very concerned for your safety, which you yourself seem to disregard at this time. You leave me no choice but to insist you no longer attempt to walk or stand." Mom wasn't allowed to move at all, unless someone held on to her.

She hated that wheelchair, naming it "Abominable Object." She hated everyone who forced it on her, too. Me, Murbeth, William, and Cassandra—all of us had become the enemy, and we were the only people she had left. We lectured and scolded her all the time. "Don't stand up!" was all anyone ever said to her anymore. Even Walter, usually the odd man out, was on our side for a change.

Finally, Mom couldn't take it anymore. Crushed and defeated, she surrendered. She went psychically limp, sitting mutely in the chair and responding to all of us with "Whatever you say." She refused to make contact with me or anyone else.

It was creepy. Mom resisted no one, ventured no opinions, and didn't care if she lived or died. You could have stuck her in a corner and left her there all day facing the wall, without hearing a word out of her. She ate the food we placed in front of her, watched the shows Walter put on the TV, listened to Wanda read, and accepted Felicia's massages. She even let Murbeth put a diaper on her, a long-standing goal for Murbeth, who could now relax about getting Mom to the toilet. I found this all exasperating and infuriating.

The only person who didn't mind was Walter. "Well, it sure is peaceful around here," he said.

Mother's attitude was suffocating. She exported her emptiness, until everyone felt just as hopeless and depressed as she did, making each day a pointless, forced march. No one was having any fun. I wracked my brain and came up with nothing: no remedy, no course of action. Day fell upon day with a thud.

But Cassandra hatched a plan.

"Let her have a drink," Cassandra said.

"Oh, come on!" I retorted. I was really proud of myself for getting Mom's drinking down to nil—revenge for all those years stuck with the unpredictable, glassy-eyed substitute mom who took over after two drinks. I, in my powerful role as boss, had finally put a stop to all that. "You can't be serious," I said.

I loved the empty liquor cabinet. Every time I opened the little wooden doors and saw nothing but ginger ale, I smiled. No more happy hour in this house. As ugly as it was, I liked punishing her. Not only that—it was for her own good.

"Oh, so you still thinking if she doesn't drink, she recover?" said

Cassandra, her hands on her hips, daring me to rationalize my edict of deprivation. I knew that from a facts-and-information point of view, my mother's condition was hopeless, irreversible. But no matter what the facts were, I found it really hard to face up to them. With Cassandra glaring at me, it might be time to admit a drink or two wouldn't make any difference.

"One little treat. Come on! A glass of wine with her dinner and her smile will come back," Cassandra said.

I gave in. This was the Departure Lounge, after all. First you do everything you can to get your mother dried out for her health and well-being. Then, to improve her quality of life, you abruptly about-face and beg her to drink.

Cassandra out-bossed me. We brokered a deal. She would hide the bottle so Walter wouldn't get manipulated into serving his Bride extra libations. "I'll tell Addie she has to keep it a secret," Cassandra said. "She'll love that!" Cassandra danced around the house until dinnertime, bursting with anticipation. She was so excited and pleased with herself, I knew I'd never have the upper hand again, if I ever had it in the first place.

"Addie, oh, Miz Addie, I have a little treat for you," Cassandra sang at dinner that night, placing a glass of Beaujolais in front of Mom, who stared blankly ahead. "Don't you want to try it?"

"Whatever you say," Mom said, dutifully picking up the glass and taking a sip. Her face didn't change, but her eyes lit up. She looked like she was afraid if she said anything, we'd realize our blunder and take it away.

"What's my Bride having?" asked Walter.

"Grape juice," Cassandra and I said simultaneously.

"I'll pass," said Walter. "I am partial to this ginger ale."

Mom put down her half-empty glass and broke into a real smile, the first one I'd seen in months. "That really is my favorite," she said, beaming. "Good old grape juice!"

Chapter Eight

FALLING APART

Give or take a glass of wine, life in the Lounge finally settled into an ironclad routine, the care-plan equivalent of reinforced concrete. Breakfast, lunch, dinner, and bedtime punctuated by Felicia, Wanda, and trips to the doctor kept Addie and Walter safe and sound. But no amount of concrete and rebar could keep them from falling apart.

Conversations with Mother became more difficult than ever because she now coughed when she tried to talk. She also choked on liquids. To prevent choking, a thickening agent was added to all her beverages, including the Beaujolais, making them the consistency of gruel. Although her "good old grape juice" now tasted terrible, I noticed Mom was asking for refills and Cassandra, out of pity, was giving in.

Walter had taken to rumbling through his possessions, scratching around, searching. He emptied his drawers, flinging socks, underpants, shirts, sweaters, and pajamas into a wild pile on his bed, then couldn't remember doing it.

After a bout of ransacking, Walter scowled, first with confusion, then outrage. "Say, who's been in my room?" he said, eying Jeffrey with suspicion.

"Talk to Daisy, Mr. Huber," Jeffrey suggested.

"The authorities will be informed," said Walter, shuffling toward the kitchen. Jeffrey ducked into the bedroom behind his back. By now, it was common household practice to engage Walter elsewhere while Jeffrey refolded the clothes and restored the room to order.

"Did you go into my private things?" Walter asked Daisy, who stood in the kitchen ironing.

"Now, Mr. Huber," said Daisy, putting down her iron. "You know I only go into your room to put your clean shirts away. You know I do that."

Walter looked at Daisy very hard, trying to follow what she was saying. "Yes, I do know that, but what of all the . . ." Walter waved his hands, unable to find the words.

Daisy was so much shorter than Walter, she had to tip her head back to talk to him. Her upturned face, sweet and kind, made Walter relax, possibly because she was always so gentle with him.

"Why don't you show me what you mean, so I can help you?"

Jeffrey had by this time reappeared and sat down quietly at the glass kitchen table.

Walter slowly turned and said, "This Daisy is going to help."

"That's good, Mr. Huber," Jeffrey said. "Don't let Daisy pull anything funny on you."

"No, no," said Walter, "not Daisy."

Jeffrey then enjoyed a nice half hour staring out the window, while Daisy gave Walter a tour of his room.

"These are your suits here, see?"

"Yes, those look like mine," Walter said, concentrating on this crucial information.

"And these are your shirts, see? Right in the drawer," said Daisy.

"Ah, so." Walter straightened up. "Well, I thank you, and I'd like to give you a little something for your time," he said, shuffling away.

"He's looking for a dollar," Daisy told me. "Sometimes he wants to tip me, like he's in a hotel." Daisy went after him. "Here, Mr. Huber, this is what you want."

Daisy handed Walter a dollar bill, the one he'd given her just a few days before.

"Yes, that," Walter said, taking the money. A moment later, he puzzled, "Now, what is this for?" scrutinizing George Washington's stony visage.

"You want to give that to Jeffrey. He in the kitchen."

"The kitchen? Ah, so." And Walter shuffled off again.

Daisy and I watched as, halfway to the kitchen, Walter came to a stop. Shaking his head with confusion, he sighed, fished out his wallet, and carefully put the money away.

According to Daisy, a few days earlier Walter defecated just inside the bathroom door, missing the toilet by a long shot, then trailed feces across the hall to his bedroom. Outraged when he noticed, he fetched Daisy to come and look. "What kind of a person would come into my house and do *that*?" Walter asked Daisy.

"No one you know," she said.

He wrote a note for Jeffrey, "Someone made a mess. Please clean it up," and painstakingly folded the paper exactly in half.

"I'll make sure he gets it," Daisy said.

Not all of Walter's correspondence reached its destination.

"Look at this," Luanne said, showing me a bunch of letters. The situation came back to me as I read them.

One evening many years ago, long before Walter was diagnosed with dementia, William was visiting for dinner. After the main course, Mother asked Walter, "Would you like ice cream with your fruit?" Walter turned bright red and roared, "*No one wants that!*" and pounded the table with his fist. Mother, totally rattled, dropped the serving dish and burst into tears.

"Don't yell at her!" William roared back.

Walter wilted instantly. "What am I supposed to say?"

"Say, 'No, thank you'!"

We didn't know, back then, that Walter had Alzheimer's, and we thought he was just an ogre. In an effort to protect Mom, William wrote Walter a very formal letter, accusing him of damaging his marriage through his thoughtless, selfish, indulgent behavior and his belittling of the Bride he'd promised to love and honor. But Walter never mentioned it, and William never knew if he'd gotten it.

As it turned out, Walter had received William's letter, and he had replied—three times. But he got the address wrong all three times, and Walter's notes came back—to wind up stuffed out of sight in Walter's desk drawer, where they rattled around for years.

In the first, he apologized for not replying, but in subsequent drafts, perhaps to hide his fraying memory, Walter rather crankily pointed out that William had failed to date his correspondence. Otherwise the tone was courtly, if not exactly humble. He broke the ice by praising William's tidy typing and then, rather abruptly, took the blame for his tantrums, though he did try to lighten things up a bit with a few exclamation points: "I'm indebted to you!" "Thank you for speaking out!" "Your letter has served its purpose well!"

Three letters, accepting blame and asking for forgiveness and guidance, laboriously written out in Walter's increasingly frail and tiny hand—I was astonished and sad. Where had this vulnerable, sensitive fellow been while the violent, bullying Walter that I despised was wreaking havoc in Addie's life? When, in Walter's life, had he disappeared? Because during the same time frame that he'd expressed his remorse and declared his love, he had continued to be as scary and unpredictable as he had been up to the present.

Of late, Walter was increasingly disturbed by a stranger who popped up unexpectedly, most often at night as Walter prepared for bed. "I don't know what that character wants," Walter complained. "I have no privacy from the likes of him!" And he pointed to the man in the mirror.

The person living in Walter's clothes these days was not fit to stand trial—no matter how satisfying it would have been to convict him for Mother's unhappiness and decline.

– – – – – –

Mother's mental biceps were withering. One morning, she reclined among the lacy pillows on her chaise with a book on her lap, which I didn't bother to mention was upside down. From the cluttered table next to her, I pulled out an address book full of people I'd never heard of.

"Hey, Mom, who is this guy?"

"Oh, he's dead," Mother said, perking up with interest.

"Mother, being alive is a basic requirement for being in an address book."

"I suppose in this you are right."

"Dead people don't have addresses, and you can't get in touch with them, at least not by conventional methods."

"The dead ones always come late," Mother said, veering into the underbrush. But I tried to play along.

"Very inconsiderate, the dead."

"No manners at all," Mother said, getting in the spirit.

"Shall I cross him off?"

"That's what he deserves! Please do!" Then she went a step further and began rating the living.

"Mr. Birch?"

"Take him off the list!"

"Deceased?"

"No, inattentive and rude," she said. "Crummy friend."

"Take that!" I said, obliterating him. "No Christmas card for you! Okay, next. How about Mrs. Charles McGraine?"

"She is a camel," Mother declared. I remembered the woman in question, her limpid eyes and pendulous upper lip. She was nice enough, but now that Mother mentioned it, she did remind me exactly of a camel. Even at this late stage, Mother's unsparing accuracy was a bit frightening.

Mom had no idea who some of these people were anymore, so I phoned and politely inquired, "Do you know Addie Henry Huber?"

One guy turned out to be the TV repairman. "Hope the TVs are okay. Give Mrs. Huber my best!" he said.

"Attentive repairman" went under his name.

Thus, we spent a happy hour sitting in judgment of those Mother had known—although her address book, once crammed with the snobby elite, was dwindling down to repairmen.

Then out of nowhere, Mom said, "Your father arrives when I least expect him."

Loop de doop.

"How does he look?"

"Wearing a tie," Mom said.

"Really! Does he send his regards to Walter?" I couldn't resist asking.

"What he says, we know not of."

That was hard to refute.

I could not imagine Dad in the afterlife. You forget that Heaven could be a complicated place if all your loved ones were in residence, ties or no ties. Was Daddy running around with Daphne? Or how about Walter's dead wife? If so, I could only hope he was having more fun than Addie was having with Walter.

Despite all the protective measures we'd painstakingly erected in the Departure Lounge, nothing could keep Mother from sabotaging herself. During that first summer, she'd single-handedly planned her own elaborate eighty-second birthday party—complete with catered lunch, flower arrangements, and cake. She remembered all that just fine; she just forgot to invite any guests. The real-life version of the nightmare party where no one shows up—Mom was brokenhearted and took to bed. When I phoned to say Happy Birthday, she refused to take my call, convinced I had simply not bothered to come.

Once when Mom and Dad were attending a chemical-industry convention, she got stranded without her luggage. And of course everyone noticed her outfit—a navy wool crepe dress with matching jacket—at the luncheon, because my father was presiding, and gave the opening address. But Addie did not panic. In those days, proper stores were closed on Sundays, but she snagged a fake pearl necklace and a spool of gold cloth ribbon from the gift shop in the hotel lobby.

For the evening event, she simply turned her dress around and wore it backward, without the jacket. She created a cocktailish V-neck by unzipping it and tucking the fabric into her brassiere, secured with safety pins concealed beneath a few silk flowers handily pinched from a hallway flower arrangement. No one would ever suspect that Addie's pearls were plastic, her gold belt braided ribbon, or that her attractive décolleté costume was a dress worn backward.

You have to be pretty intact to pull off shaking hands in a receiving line for hours in this getup. But those days were gone. Now Mom couldn't even pull off a birthday party. Her guest list was lost in the deepening confusion at the Departure Lounge.

On September 11, 2001, a friend called to say, "A plane crashed into the World Trade Center!" At first, I didn't believe her, but when the second tower was hit, the world went on *tilt*. It's hard to remember, now that 9/11 is encoded in our memories, that we had no idea what was happening at the time. It was all chaos, uncertainty, and fear.

I was desperately worried about Mom and Walter, who lived twelve miles from the World Trade Center. Would bombs rain down on Oldhill? Were the old people and their caregivers all right? Were Cassandra, Murbeth, and Jeffrey still showing up? I imagined Mom collapsed and helpless in the bathroom, Walter running off through an unlocked door.

Though Cathy reported that the old people were carrying on as usual, I felt compelled to see for myself. As soon as the airspace opened up, I got on a Continental jet headed for Newark. My husband was furious. "You have no idea if it's safe! What if the airspace is shut down again? You could be gone for weeks! Who'll take care of the kids?" But I knew that with Rob to watch out for them, our children would be safe. I couldn't be sure if Addie and Walter were. So I made the calls, got the babysitters lined up, and called the dog walker. I prepared meals and froze them. I got on the plane.

The outside world might have been incredibly changed, but as Cathy had said, life at the Departure Lounge was pretty much the same. Cassandra, Murbeth, and Jeffrey occupied the kitchen. Both parents were stationed before the blasting TV, watching footage of the collapsing towers, over and over. But each time Walter saw it, it was breaking news to him.

"We're under attack!" he announced every five minutes, unable to absorb the rattling newscasts. Each time, he was shocked, afraid, and then angry. "I need a gun to protect my Bride," he said, "because those others"—waving a hand toward the kitchen—"can't do it like I can." He held out his arm, pointing his finger like a kid about to say, "Bang!"

"Yes," said my mother, "and soon the whole city will be destroyed." She seemed rather matter-of-fact, as if to say, "So, what else is new?" Then I realized she'd been watching the footage for days because there was nothing else on TV.

No matter how many times I told them what had happened—the hijacked planes, the box cutters, the Twin Towers, the Pentagon, the Pennsylvania crash—Walter couldn't absorb the facts.

"Pennsylvania? All the way out there?" Walter said. "I thought it was here in New York. What are they talking about a place like Pennsylvania for?"

He flicked to another channel: more towers collapsing, more fleeing crowds. "Look! We're under attack!" he shouted.

I hadn't the slightest idea of how to help Addie and Walter understand events that I couldn't grasp myself, along with the rest of the world. There was no way to put this disaster in perspective or to relieve my parents' agitation. So I squeezed Walter's hand, and I kissed the top of Mom's head, as long ago she used to kiss mine.

I turned the TV off and stuck a movie into the VCR. *Thunderhead—Son of Flicka,* a 1945 made-for-children horse story was just about right for Mom and Walter. Horses galloping around a green field under a blue sky, a kid successfully taming a wild stallion—both parents were enthralled and delighted by the wide turns of plot.

"Look—he's getting on the horse! Oops, he fell that time!" Walter delivered a steady commentary on the scenes unfolding before us. "I wonder what he's going to do now. Oh, he's getting back on!" And since Mom couldn't see, this guided tour was helpful.

But when the movie ended, the TV cut back on and the Twin

Towers collapsed. The brief *Thunderhead* respite was erased. We were "under attack!"

Finally I unplugged the set.

"Hey, this won't go on!" said Walter, shaking the remote.

"It's because of the war, dear," Mom said, coughing hard.

"What war?"

"This new war," Mother said, recovering. "Is this a war?" she asked me.

"I don't know yet, Mom," I said. "No one knows exactly what this is."

"Well, we should stock up on candles and kerosene—and gin," she added, rather gleefully.

"We'll need bottled water," said Walter, thinking hard.

"Yes, and corned beef hash!" Mother's eyes gleamed. "And gin!"

"I've always been partial to hash," Walter said. "And I like it with ketchup."

"Ketchup!" said Mom. "We must have ketchup on our list!"

"We'll need blankets," said Walter.

"We can sleep in the basement." She was excited by this plan.

"All the way down there?" said Walter, not quite liking that idea.

"Yes, because of the bombs!" Mother replied.

"Bombs!" said Walter. "I don't care for any bombs."

"Okay, no bombs," agreed Mother, "just the candles and gin. *And we can fire the help!*"

"Yes," Walter said. "We won't need them in the basement."

"No. We can just eat out of the cans and take swigs of gin!" Mother was thrilled.

"I thought I had a gun around here someplace," said Walter. "Let me call Cathy and see if she knows where it is."

Mom and Walter were not really happy about the prospect of war. They were just ready to revisit a time when they were young, vigorous, and brave. The two of them were all set to be heroic, not to mention back in control. In return, living in the basement with a candle and blanket seemed like a good deal.

My apocalyptic fears for them in the early days just after the attacks—that war was coming, that Cassandra, Jeffrey, and Murbeth would soon be wearing helmets and launching rockets as I smuggled the old people across the border to live with my family—never materialized. Instead, security lines clogged airports, American flags rippled across the land, and war came not to us, but to Iraq. Life at the Departure Lounge, facilitated by Cassandra, Murbeth, Jeffrey, and the weekend relay team, rumbled along on schedule, and surprising and surreal events continued to astound me.

Life had become one long endurance test. My husband and my children were almost out of resilience—there wasn't much stretch left in the family fiber, which had gone as far as it could to cope with my neglect. A choice between life in Nova Scotia and life at the Departure Lounge was coming up soon. I'd have to warn William that he might not be able to count on my showing up much longer.

One night—during which season I can't quite remember—I was waiting to talk to Murbeth after she and Jeffrey had finished readying Mom and Walter for bed. Restless and bored, I descended the neckbreaking basement steps—neck-breaking for anyone but Walter, that is, who once tripped and tumbled all the way to the bottom and escaped with only a few bruises.

I pulled the chain of the bare lightbulb, noting that anything kept down here for more than a month picked up the smell of a tomb.

Two pairs of skates, one black and one white, hung from a beam like relics. Mom had stopped ice-skating well before Dad died. In one corner stood an odd array of ancient stationary bikes and an antiquated rowing machine. In the early days of their marriage, when Mom was bent on improving Walter for his own good, she set up this basement "home gym." But these pathetic contraptions could not have come from any store, and I couldn't imagine Mom cruising yard sales for used equipment. Where on earth had she found them? A mystery.

Moseying around behind the elevator shaft, I came upon two storage rooms I'd forgotten about. One was jammed with William's books, curling in the damp. The other held oddments belonging to Walter, dumped there by the moving company when he moved in with

Mom: peeling golf trophies, a leather binoculars case, tennis racquets, and a box of wooden tees. A golf bag draped in cobwebs leaned against the wall. On closer inspection, it contained two old shirts, a tire iron, and some rat poison.

I was about to turn out the light and depart when I noticed a metal filing cabinet stuck in the shadows. It was all too possible that some crucial document like the deed to the house was in there, so I hauled the rusty drawers open for a quick look.

The top drawer contained a bunch of old stationery with Walter's former address and a flashlight leaking battery acid. The bottom drawer was crammed with an old sweater—and hiding under that moldering cardigan, in a cardboard box, was a mound of jewels.

I was bedazzled by cut and polished stones of all sizes and kinds—diamonds, rubies, emeralds, aquamarines, sapphires, tourmalines, and amethysts—carefully packaged in plastic and labeled by weight. And loose pearls, lots of them. Most were normal jewelry-size stones, but some were like the crown jewels. Of course, they could have all been fake, but they looked pretty real to me. I dug around hoping, by some miracle, to find Mom's missing loot. But her treasures were not among the spoils, which I was certain belonged to Walter, since his family tree bore a few jewelers.

The filing cabinet was unlocked, the door to the basement was unlocked, and anyone, anytime, could have grabbed a handful and walked off with a fortune. As I sat on the cold linoleum tile, the endless paradox of the Departure Lounge rolled over me. No one even knew this stuff was here. Too bad for our jewel thief, who could have snatched this conveniently bagged and tagged inventory, instead of robbing my mother, and we wouldn't have ever known.

Walter certainly wouldn't have known. He was upstairs entering sweepstakes while his legitimate nest egg languished in the basement beneath his feet—utterly forgotten. I called Cathy that same night and asked her to take the plunder away. I didn't want to expose myself or the staff to any liability. With relief, I handed her a large plastic shopping bag stuffed with riches and never heard another word.

The short days and long nights brought with them a sad season to the Departure Lounge. The staff kept Walter and Addie cooped up in the house, allegedly so they wouldn't catch cold, but more likely, they wanted to avoid the hassle. At Thanksgiving, Addie was so unmoored she dispensed with her knife and fork to eat with her bare hands. At Christmastime, Cathy valiantly attempted a festive dinner. Walter happily put on a red elf hat, but Addie, confused and assuming that she was supposed to be the hostess, was upset by her status as a guest. January and February slowly crawled along, with no end in sight, and nothing to look forward to.

One afternoon I sat next to Mother on the little wicker couch, with my arm around her. The new upholstery I'd paid for had still not arrived, and I didn't know how much longer I could stand these yellow-stained cushions.

Walter was riveted to a golf game. Cassandra banged pots around in the kitchen, busy and laughing with Murbeth and Jeffrey. I felt left out of the party, and it occurred to me that Mom, stuck in front of a golf game she couldn't see, probably did, too. She'd have had fun in the kitchen, but she wouldn't leave Walter all by himself, even though he'd begun to doze, listing rather precariously over the side of his chair. I picked up the remote and turned the sound off.

She turned and glared at me. "What am I now? I used to be in charge. Now people won't even let me *walk*!" Mom wiped her nose with her twisted hand, and I gave her a tissue that got uselessly trapped between her knuckles. She couldn't see the tears brimming in my eyes.

She plucked and tugged at my sleeve. "Tell me how I can live when I can't do a thing."

What could I say? How does one live when the end of life is in sight, but hasn't yet arrived? Nobody tells you this stuff. But shouldn't a lifetime of church on Sunday offer some comfort, especially now?

"What about God?"

Mom's body next to mine was rigid. Clutching my arm so hard it hurt, she shook her head. "God isn't working anymore."

I wanted to help her so badly, but Mom wouldn't buy dumb platitudes. No Kahlil Gibran for her. I struggled, patched together words that couldn't bear the weight and came apart before I could say them. We sat in silence.

Outside, the sun dropped below the ridge. Suddenly a sparkling yellow and blue pattern appeared on the wall, flickering—the fleeting vision you don't see because it isn't on the agenda, the great, incidental stuff that makes life worth living.

Then it faded and was gone. Every day has its beauty, but it's easy to miss.

I took a breath and spoke. "For years you had a great time bossing everyone around. And you were good at it, Mom. But you can't be in charge anymore. That's over. Still, a house full of people are here every day—Cassandra, Murbeth, Jeffrey, and the others. Let it mean something. Make it count. Thank them when they help you, even though you really wish you could do everything yourself. Make their time worthwhile. Accept their presence as a gift."

She looked at me wordlessly, as though this talking-to showed her how little I knew.

"Mom, the alternative is bitterness." She turned away, the American eagle, old and defeated.

I felt awful. So preachy and presumptuous. I should have just told her how I loved her.

The next day I flew home to Halifax to my children, the laundry, and the bills. As I stumbled into the kitchen with my suitcase and the groceries I'd picked up on the way back from the airport, the phone rang. It was Mom, direct from the dinner table, the cutlery clanking against the plates, Cassandra in the background, telling Mom how to hold the phone.

"Darling? Walter and I are enjoying such a good dinner that Cassandra has made. And I want to say thank you to her, and a thank you to you."

Though her cheerful tone sounded forced, I knew she'd heard me and she was trying. I so hoped it made a difference. And I hope I remember my great advice when I need a helper in the bathroom.

Mom's coughing and choking got worse. In June, Cassandra and I wrestled the Abominable Object into the car and took Mom to the hospital for an ultrasound of her heart. Decked out in a blue straw hat covered with red flowers, Mom waved and smiled like the Queen of England, through miles of hospital corridors, up elevators, down elevators, and into a windowless cinder-block waiting room, where we sat for hours. Cassandra fell asleep while I read aloud, for Mother's benefit, six issues of *Reader's Digest.*

Finally it was our turn. Cassandra and I didn't leave the testing suite, though the technician clearly wanted us in the waiting room, where we belonged. I guess she couldn't stand up to the two of us, formidable as we were.

Mom lay on the gurney, unself-consciously stripped to the waist. When you've been naked and washed by complete strangers, you'll take your clothes off in front of anyone.

Black-and-white shapes wavered on the video screen as the technician rolled the sensor around on Mom's chest.

"Mrs. Huber, did you have rheumatic fever?" she asked.

Then I knew Mom was in real trouble. Rheumatic fever damages the heart valves. So unless things looked bad, there'd be no reason to ask the question. Even to my untrained eye, it was obvious that the valves, their edges frayed like an old flag, didn't close.

"They trying to shake hands but don't reach," Cassandra said, which was exactly so.

The blood backwashed and the heart couldn't keep up with the flow. Mom had congestive heart failure, which makes you tired and makes you cough. Over time, her battered old heart was going to give out.

Don't get me wrong. The good part of Mom's life was shrinking down to nothing, and the hard parts were about all that remained. So I didn't long for a cure, nor did I expect one. Those who live long die in the end. But Addie was my compass north; as long as she was around, I knew where I was, even if I was running in the opposite direction. How would I get my bearings without her?

We got Mom dressed, thanked the lady, and went home to wait.

Once again late for my plane, I was rushing out of the Devonshire Inn when the owner nabbed me. "Say, you're from Canada, right? Wait right here!" and he disappeared, to return with a brown paper bag. "I've been saving these quarters for years. Canadian. Worthless. You may as well have them," he said, thrusting fifteen pounds of rolled coins into my hands. What could I possibly say but "Thank you!"? I ran for the car, hoping to make it to the airport in time.

I was hoisting my bag onto the conveyer belt when I remembered the quarters. "There's all this change in the outside pocket . . ." I made a motion to unzip it.

"Don't touch the bag, ma'am," the security attendant barked.

"But there's all . . ."

"Don't touch the bag."

Nearby passengers turned to look. A little frisson of interest rippled around me.

My bag, loaded with what I was sure would look on the X-ray like pipe bombs, disappeared through the rubber curtain. The belt made a clanking noise, and my transparent suitcase crossed the screen, showing five solid bars. "Over there," the attendant directed me. My bag disappeared with a handler.

"Here!" said a man, with my bag on a table in front of him like a magician. "Sit," he said, pointing to a chair. The soldiers standing behind me on a gray rubber mat perked up. They'd seen this a thousand times, but you never knew.

In full view of the public, the bag-search man yanked the zipper and pulled out the coins, which he set aside. Then he opened a ball of socks, felt the underwire in my bra. I didn't say a word. He had rules to follow.

Then he pulled out a naked tampon. "And what is this?" he demanded, holding it up for all to see.

A lot more people were looking my way than I'd realized. The crowd burst out laughing. Even the soldiers snickered on their mat.

I didn't know where this man was from or what cultural taboos shaped his ideas about women. I do know he couldn't have been in the West for too long, because he'd have learned about tampons just from watching TV. I also knew he was weary and didn't want to lose his job.

"That is a toiletry," I told him, looking him square in the eye. The man turned it over in his hand. The soldiers were now laughing out loud, and the man looked at me, puzzled.

"A what?"

I looked at him very, very hard. *"A toiletry."*

"Okay." He blinked, lowering the tampon from view. "You have a good trip." His voice was devoid of expression, but he gave me an immensely grateful look. He knew, as we say in America, I saved his ass.

Past the soldiers was the Meditation Room. I'd never seen anyone else in there, though on my constant travels, I'd taken to stopping in to collect myself and to reflect on these flights from one world to another.

The rows of chairs stood empty. Draping a windowless wall was a blue curtain, behind which was a sort of portable altar. A large vase of fake flowers rested in a niche. A sign said to please remove my shoes out of deference to Muslims. A prayer rug commanded the back corner, beside a huge compass indicating east. Another sign informed me that Mass was celebrated every day at 9 A.M. A visit with a rabbi can be arranged.

And if religion doesn't appeal to you, there is a small shrine to New Jersey, with a flag, a plastic poinsettia, and a message from the governor wishing you well on your journey through the Garden State.

Here the world's great religions are stripped down to fit and are accommodated with little effort—possibly an afterthought on the part of the airport architects—in this dim, anonymous room.

Back in the terminal, I sat down, sighed, and waited for my flight. My life was on hold—a fractured mess. The only things keeping chaos at bay were my notebooks: one for Halifax, one for Oldhill. They reminded me where I was and what I had to worry about. The driving momentum of ever-growing lists had become a way of life.

You get used to it. You even get good at it. You forget that, at some point, everything will change.

Chapter Nine

LAST CALL

I just happened to call that Saturday morning. Althea, one of the temps, answered the phone. "Well, they told me not to come on Sunday and now people want to know why I wasn't . . ." Althea mumbled. A loud commotion in the background made it almost impossible to understand her.

"What's all that racket?" I shouted into the phone. I heard the doorbell ring, and then a lot of shuffling, clanging, and muffled voices.

Althea started in again. "Marilyn says people was upset I didn't come on Sunday but nobody told me nothing about . . ." The shuffling got louder.

"Althea, I didn't talk to Marilyn. What is going on?"

"Marilyn right here. You can talk to her yourself." Althea put her hand over the phone and after a long, staticky interlude, Marilyn got on the line.

"Maybe I can call you back because—"

At that moment, Walter roared in the background, "You can't take my wife!"

Marilyn yelled at Walter, "Mr. Huber, I am obligated by the laws of the State of New Jersey to remove your wife because of her condition. Now, do you want me to call the police, or will you calm yourself and let me do my job?" She put the phone down.

A male voice said, "One, two, and three," followed by a big thud. I could hear Althea rambling on: ". . . so I said I'd come in, but since no one needed no meal and my kids wanted me to stay because their dad was bringing the TV . . ."

Marilyn picked up the phone again. "The ambulance is here. Your mother is unresponsive and I'm taking her to the hospital. We'll call you from there." And she hung up on me. I waited for an hour, but she didn't call back.

I phoned William, but Cassandra had already called. "I changed my ticket," he said. "What about the others?" We had all planned to show up for Mom's eighty-third birthday party, which she'd planned herself, months in advance. This time, she'd sent out invitations with RSVPs (in Luanne's steady handwriting). The flowers, the luncheon, and the rentals were all paid for. She even had a new outfit, mail-order from Talbot's—but now this "development," whatever it was.

I sat dumbly in my kitchen like I'd been whacked in the head with a frying pan, my toast cold, and rain pounding on the window. Should I keep going with the grocery shopping and soccer-team carpool or initiate the emergency alert sequence?

Here's a little advice. Never, ever go into the hospital over the weekend if you can help it, because they can't really do anything except prevent you from dying immediately. They pump you full of drugs, drip fluids into your arm, put oxygen tubes in your nose, and wait for Monday. There is no one on site to diagnose, prognose, or read MRIs—and no one's coming in off the ninth hole for a sick old lady who collapsed on a Saturday morning.

Once again, I had no definitive information. If Mom wasn't really dying, I didn't want to go since I was already scheduled to leave in less than a week—but there's no way to know. You spend years jumping on planes when it turns out you didn't need to. You buy the ticket, get the babysitter, do the shopping, arrange for the cleaning service, and write out hour-by-hour schedules for everyone's life—and after you cross off every little thing on your list, you grind your teeth and think, *This time, she better die.* And then you feel terrible.

I felt even worse when Rob said, "The garden is going to shit because you never water it, like everything else around here that you don't follow through on." He was so sick and tired of taking up the slack, he didn't seem to understand that this was probably the last trip, the last summons, the end. The past year and a half had been like chasing each other through a thicket of thornbushes. A long haul for both of us. Still, a little sympathy would have gone a long way, rather than the argument we had, yelling in the street right in front of the house, where the neighbors could hear every word clearly enough to offer coaching from the sidelines.

So I watered the garden, and stayed up all night drinking coffee, making schedules and preparing lasagna and meat loaf and tuna noodle casserole and muffins and banana bread, while Rob shook the house dragging a sofa from room to room and slamming doors. After a while, I really hoped he'd die, too. The sooner, the better. Still mad at him, I slept on the couch.

You know your mental health is precarious when you wish your husband and your mother would both die, preferably simultaneously, for your own peace of mind and convenience.

When I finally got to the hospital, it was almost dawn. Mom lay on the bed under a buzzing fluorescent light. Her name, spelled wrong, was scribbled on a piece of paper taped to the wall. I dumped my suitcase on the floor and flipped through her chart, but the diagnosis and prognosis sections were blank, confirmed by a bunch of illegible signatures at the bottom. West Palm Beach all over again.

A gasping inhalation shook her, and then the breath reversed and rushed out. I didn't know if she was conscious. "Mom, you look like a million bucks in that hospital gown," I said, kissing her.

She grimaced harder and rasped, "Green is not entirely my color," without opening her eyes. I laughed and kissed her again. Mom did not look too good. Her hair stuck out like pinfeathers. A deep, ponderous frown forked between her eyes, which were clamped shut. A faint trace of lipstick clung to her mouth. She looked like she might die any second. But I'd thought that before and been wrong.

Mom's room was partitioned by a curtain. A loud voice on the other side squawked, "Get me a doctor! I'm dying in here! Nurse! Fifteen, forty-four, nineteen twenty-five, dying. The pain, the pain! A nurse!"

Mom opened one eye. "She's a screamer," she said matter-of-factly.

I peeked around the curtain. There, in a tangle of sheets and tubing, sat Hettie Pryde, according to the label stuck to the wall over her head. "Ninety-nine, nineteen forty-five, twenty-two and a half," Hettie said by way of introduction. "Are you a doctor?" Hettie had long gray hair, and was completely naked except for a diaper.

"No."

"Get me a doctor! Twenty-two thousand, three hundred ninety-seven times twenty is not enough!"

A nurse came running in. "Hettie, stop that yelling. What's bothering you now?"

Hettie smiled gleefully because she'd made the nurse come, and then whined, "My back itches."

I returned to Mother, curled up like a shrimp, her breath rattling in and out. I shook her shoulder, but she didn't wake up.

As the morning wore on, the faithful began to trickle in. Murbeth and Cassandra continued to come to work—no work, no pay—and showed up for their shifts here, where there was nothing for them to do.

Although my mother was almost comatose, the hospital continued to send her large quantities of terrible meals. Trays of pizza, hamburgers, and waffles took up valuable counter space next to her bed.

Fortunately, Murbeth possessed an unassailable love of food, and set herself the task of coping with this useless abundance. Sidling over to a fresh arrival, Murbeth lifted the tan plastic cover and sniffed. "Now, let me just look at this, since Mother not having any . . ." Cassandra watched and shook her head.

Then Alice arrived, pulling her raincoat tight around her like a blanket. She'd dropped everything when Addie was admitted, and, after staying up all night, was worn out from the stress and confusion, not to mention Hettie's yelling.

"I think she's going to pull out of this one," said Cassandra, looking hard at Addie while Murbeth went to work on a plate of limp French toast.

"I hope you're right," Alice said, but she sounded doubtful.

A young doctor with limpid eyes wandered in, consulting his clipboard. "Could be a reaction to the antibiotic—I've seen it happen. She might go home in a few days." Score one for living.

Another doctor showed up a few minutes later, checked Mom's chart, and said, "This doesn't look good," as though referring to an expiration date. Score one for dying.

Then the floor nurse took me aside and said, "If it was my mom? I'd tell my family to get here."

I didn't have to. Everyone changed their plans and flew in a week early. Poor Mom, after all her careful party preparations. She had to be furious. But, as Mom had said when Dad died in the airport, the timing was almost convenient, really.

A day later, it was standing room only in Mom's hospital room. In addition to Murbeth, Cassandra, Daisy, Luanne, Alice, William, and me, Sophie arrived from L.A. with her teenage daughter, and Roland and his wife, from Nova Scotia. There was nothing to do but add more seats to the growing line of plastic chairs along the wall.

"What day is it?" asked Mom, clawing her way back to consciousness for a moment.

"July 4, 1932!" yelled Hettie. "January 1, 1929!" Hettie was not helping to clarify the situation.

"It's Monday morning, Mom."

"I saw a very small person," Mom said. "Who is me."

A near-death experience? I'd heard that people brought back from the brink in the ER or the ambulance often observe themselves being shocked back to life, as though looking down from the ceiling.

"Are you in pain? Does anything hurt?" Alice asked.

"Only my head," Mom said, and she slipped away again.

Mom slept while Hettie yelled until I went over to her side of the room.

"I've got cancer," Hettie said, "and I am ninety-eight years old. It just can't kill me."

"Good for you," I said.

"Where's my mother?"

"Hettie, if you are ninety-eight, I presume she's dead."

"Yes, that's right."

After we got that straightened out, I smoothed Hettie's long hair from her forehead.

"That's nice, that's Mama," said Hettie. "I knew she was around here."

Everyone took a break for lunch, but I was too anxious to join them. I didn't want to leave Addie for an instant.

A new doctor arrived and pinched Mom's toes so hard she yelped, suddenly wide awake. "You'll need some rehab, Adelaide," he said. "But we'll have you walking in no time." These people knew nothing, and they never talked to one another. And no one had called Addie by her full name since *her* mother died.

Finally Mom's doctor, a rumpled, overweight man with dirty glasses, beckoned me to the hallway. He didn't put too fine a point on the situation. "The clot will put pressure on parts of her brain, which will then die and necrotize. Her basic metabolic functions will fail, and her lungs will fill with fluid."

"Your colleagues say otherwise."

He smiled, not unkindly. "I have the MRI. There's a chance her heart will fail first, of course."

"How long?" I asked him.

"If you keep her here, with an IV, maybe two weeks. No fluids, maybe five days."

Bleed in brain, blood clot, dead. I didn't feel shocked or like crying.

"When can we get out of here?" I asked him. Well, he had to do the swallow test and the oxygen test, and get the discharge plan together. And there were forms to sign. Then he asked me if I wanted hospice.

We had three home health-care aides, one a nurse. What did we need hospice for?

"Advice and support?" the doctor said, shrugging.

I didn't want any goddamn advice and I had plenty of support, so I said no. That was very dumb of me, and that doctor should have probed, but maybe he didn't know much about death.

If you are dying at home, I suggest you get hospice services, because you cannot get drugs without a doctor, and you will need drugs. Hospice gives you access to morphine.

Back in the room, Hettie was counting by fives, mercifully not too loudly, while Mom lay panting on her bed.

"Mom, you're dying," I said.

She opened her eyes wide and said, "Really?"

"Yes, really."

Mom rose up a little. "I am delighted," she said. This was good news.

"Do you want to go home, or stay in the hospital?"

"Home," she said. "In my own bed."

By the time everyone had returned from lunch, I was already lining up the ambulance.

There were three miracles connected to Mom's final curtain.

First, Walter wound up in the hospital, too. He'd been doing poorly since his Bride left. He'd fainted and fallen and then popped up right down the hall, heavily sedated and tied into bed. Because his fever spiked, a cold blanket, which is the opposite of a hot-water bottle, covered him from his neck to his feet. He recognized me, but didn't know who I was. "Oh, hello," said Walter. "What a surprise."

Jeffrey was sound alseep in a chair next to Walter's bed. I kicked the bottom of his foot. "Don't sleep with your mouth open, Jeffrey. Every old person on this ward is sleeping with his mouth open. You want to get tied to a bed?"

Jeffrey laughed. "Only by you."

"Mom's going home to die," I said, and Jeffrey bowed his head, hugging his elbows. Walter snored and the TV flickered like Christmas tinsel.

"If he get out, how that going to work?" he asked me.

The house would be full of family, coming and going, and Walter hated confusion. I could see it—the yelling, the fisticuffs, the disapproving police officers. Not your ideal final days of peace and quiet. Not only that, someone unfamiliar with the protocols of the Departure Lounge was bound to leave a door open, and Walter would wander off in search of a liquor store. A nightmare. I couldn't cope with Walter.

The discharge nurse had two laptops, two cell phones, a regular phone, and a pager. Her hair was perfect.

"Sit. Talk," she said, pointing to a chair. I tried to explain, but life at the Departure Lounge really made no sense at all. "So, let me get this. You want the husband out of the way so the mom can die in peace?" Sad but true. I nodded, and the nurse shook her head in disbelief.

"How long?" she asked, scribbling on a pad. When I didn't answer right away, she said sharply, "How long till Mom dies?"

"They said five days."

"Okay. You were never here. Out."

"Thank you," I said.

"Out." She pointed to the door.

I had to sign a bunch more papers, including one saying that said we would not show up in the emergency room to get Mom readmitted, because Mom chose death. I knew Mom wanted to go home to die; she'd told me for years and years. But I found it hard, very hard, to grasp the pen and scribble my name on that line.

Absent Walter, the usual maximum-security procedures at Mom's house weren't necessary. Doors and windows were opened, admitting the hot August air, and sweet summer sounds flooded the house—birds, lawn mowers, and children. The smell of cut grass and hot pavement fumigated the musty, cloying rooms. I cut roses in the yard, the Peace roses grafted from my father's favorite bush from the old house, and I arranged vases in Mom's room, hoping for a decorative rather than funerary touch.

Murbeth, Cassandra, and I washed Mom up, combed her hair, and helped her into a fresh yellow silk and lace gown, one of her favorites. Propped up on the pillows rather grandly, she was ready to hold court and enjoy this new turn of events. "Bring in the guests," she said, squinting as though in the sun.

My cousin Olive was the first to arrive. For most of her sixty years, Olive had rarely fit in. But she'd found acceptance and stability in a small Christian sect. As an expression of her newfound faith, she wore a Mennonite-style kerchief covering her pale hair. Olive was a very solid woman.

"Can I see Aunt Addie?" she asked in a teeny voice, too small to be emanating from such bulk. At that exact same moment, Monique Johnson, the florist's wife, scurried like a crab through the front door, straight into Mother's bedroom, and hopped up onto the bed. "Praise the Lord!" said Monique. Olive and Monique looked at each other with the light of recognition, and they both began to pray loudly. Mother opened her eyes, astonished to find them there. "You are going to Jesus," Monique said.

"Aunt Addie, don't be afraid," Olive told her, lumbering onto the bed with Monique and taking Mother's desiccated hand.

I got the impression Mom was more frightened of this impromptu prayer meeting than she was of dying. "The Lord is my shepherd; I shall not want," began Olive.

"He maketh me to lie down in green pastures," answered Monique.

I decided four was a crowd at this party and gently backed out of the room. Dying or not, Mom would have to fend for herself in the company of the Self-Chosen.

The driveway resembled a used-car lot as a cast of many assembled for this increasingly odd event. Alice; Sophie with her daughter; Roland and his wife; Danny, my cousin from Florida; and Daisy, Luanne, and Cassandra all showed up, hungry. Corks popped, glasses clinked. William put on an apron and dedicated himself to dinner for twelve with candles, flowers, and homemade meatballs. As we dished up the plates, we got the surprise of a lifetime. Cassandra wheeled Mother into the kitchen. "Addie wants to come, too. She's lonely in the bedroom!"

The doctors said Mom would never eat again, that she could barely swallow, that she was basically as good as dead. But she had a different plan. Mom—in her favorite wide-brimmed black hat, blue silk dress, and pearls—made the comeback of the century. Cassandra had even stuck high heels on her skinny old feet. She looked a bit vague, but smiled all around, the life of the party. Her surreal reprieve raised a few false hopes, a wild swelling in the chest. Maybe the MRI was really someone else's. Maybe she'd survive this stroke and go on to live a few happy, Walter-free years in the bosom of the family. But part of me, the part that knew it was a dream, just wanted to wake up and get this dying thing back on track.

If you had chanced to look through the kitchen window—that is, if you had a stepladder and climbed over the thornbush—you'd have seen a large family crowded around a table, faces illuminated by candlelight, smears of red sauce on a few chins. And you'd have heard the entire songbooks of *The Sound of Music* and *Peter Pan* sung in three-part harmony, in duets, in rounds, with a smattering of hymns thrown in. For once we were the family we'd longed for, gathered around that table, loving, tender, and kind.

The candles burned down, the plates emptied. Cassandra and Sophie wheeled Mom away to bed. While a few inebriates warbled away over the dishes, I sat smoking out on the front steps, listening to animated sounds of cheerful domesticity that I never, in a million years, thought I'd hear coming from that house. Through the leaves of the cherry tree, the sweet old moon hanging in the sky made good company, and I lit cigarette after cigarette, though I don't normally smoke.

Sophie's voice came through the open window. "Has anyone seen Meg?" Alice and Sophie were standing at the bedside when I arrived. Mom sat leaning back on her pillows, with a crazy, ecstatic smile.

"Today I am so happy because I am dying, and now I am going to give you your rings!" Her words slurred, recalling the martini days.

I looked at Alice, she looked at me, and our eyes bulged out. *What rings?*

Mom continued. "I have been waiting for this moment!" Joy radiated from her face, as she made a swooping theatrical gesture with her hand, unfurling her fingers into a flat, outstretched palm, the kind you make when you give a horse a lump of sugar.

Mom had been anticipating this scene for decades, ever since she saw those rings in the jewelry store. Her daughters gathered at her bedside, herself in the spotlight, bestowing the royal bling as we groveled with gratitude and delight. Who cared if the rings were gone? Mom wasn't going to let a little thing like a robbery, a low-class *thief,* spoil her plans.

She leaned forward, stretching her hand toward Alice. "This one is for you, dear," and held out her empty palm.

"Wow," I said. "That ring will go with everything!"

"It sure will," said Alice, carefully taking the pretend ring and pretending to put it on. "How beautiful! And just my size."

Then Mom gave pretend rings to Sophie and to me, too. We oohed and aahed, admiring the glittering ruby, the gigantic sapphire, the bright topaz—invisible though they were. The moment was surreal, transcendental, and pure, the best "thing" my mother ever gave me.

Mother beamed, and it was all I could do not to bawl my head off. "This is the happiest day and I love you all so much," she said. And I believed her.

The next day was Mom's eighty-third birthday. Not her fancy catered party, which was still days off, but the actual date of her birth. The energy she'd had the night before was dissipating, the look in her eyes remote, fixed on some invisible horizon. Cassandra dressed her up in her favorite St. John knit suit, the green one with the scooped neckline, and Mother received the people who'd heard and come to say good-bye. I posed as a weird usherette, serving tea and coffee to help along the awkward moments, those gaps in the pretense that this was a normal, impromptu social call, and Mom was fine.

Where had all these "close friends" been when Mom was so lonely? I could barely be civil when they told me what a great person my mother was, those same damn people who wouldn't invite her for dinner after Dad died. By the end of the day, I was nasty. "Yes, we haven't seen much of you—have you been on a long trip or something? Did you move away? No? You still live down the block?"

The church people made me hopping mad. None of the devoted members of her Christian study group had had the time to read the Bible out loud to her once in a while. No wonder it seemed God quit working for Mom. His people didn't even show up.

I had a sudden inspiration to call Dr. Gage, Mom's former doctor, whom I'd had to fire because we could never get a hold of him. I wasn't surprised to find myself talking to his answering machine. "My mother, Addie Henry Huber, a former patient of yours, is pretty much on her deathbed. But she still carries a torch for you. A visit from you would mean a lot, if you could get here today."

I hung up, never dreaming that the roaring red Harley that raced up the driveway an hour later would be Dr. Gage. I was flummoxed by the tall stranger in black leather boots, until he pulled his helmet off, revealing his luxuriant wavy hair. The impervious man I'd written off looked shaken up, even unsure of himself. "I didn't even know she was sick," he said, holding out his hands, palms up.

Addie's face lit up like Christmas the instant she saw him. Rising from her deathbed, she batted her eyes at him, grinning. He sat down on the bed and took her hand—and kissed it.

I cleared the room, knowing Dr. Gage would not wish to be observed as he went to pieces. I hung out in the kitchen, catching up with Danny, whom I hadn't seen in years, until I heard the motorcycle blatter away. Dr. Gage hadn't bothered to say good-bye.

My niece made Mom a birthday cake, a good occupying project for a teenager, and in the evening, we did the dinner thing again. But the luster was gone, because undeniably the Grim Reaper was now sitting with us. Some deaf and dumb part of me wanted encore after encore of that enchanted dinner party. But Mom could hardly hold up her head. Singing "Happy Birthday" was bad enough, but then there were the presents. Handkerchiefs, a bottle of perfume, a box of note cards—what do you give someone facing the ultimate journey? A Swiss army knife, a box of matches, a roll of duct tape? Mom barely noticed when we lifted her from the chair and into her bed.

I'd moved from my room with the parking-lot view at the Devonshire Inn to the house, to Jeffrey's room, which was now empty. The agency sent a new person, a nurse named Angela, to stay in Mom's room at this dire time. Why, in the name of God, Mom had to make new acquaintances at this point, I didn't know. But that's home care in America for you. I gave Angela the tour and my routine history of the situation, chatted just enough to be polite, threw myself exhausted into bed, and plummeted into fitful sleep.

Suddenly someone was shaking me awake, proclaiming in a loud stage whisper, "She passed! Your mother, she passed!" Angela, whom I barely remembered, crouched over me in the dark. She shook me vigorously some more. I was too groggy to get it.

"Who passed what?" I asked. The little blue clock face said 2:15.

"Your mother! She passed over!"

I leaped up and ran through the kitchen, down the hall, rattling the photos along the wall, charging into Mom's room, where she was lying on her side, her eyes wide open, looking at me.

"Hi, Meggo," she said.

I stood, breathing hard, until Nurse Angela caught up. I wanted her to see this. "You aren't dead, are you, Mom?" I said with my hands on my hips.

"Nope," Mom said, though she sounded like she was talking underwater.

"Mom says she's alive," I said to Angela, who slunk and cringed until I threw a pillow at her. Mom gurgled out a laugh. Here at the Departure Lounge, we can relate to little errors like that, because sometimes it is very hard to tell the living from the dead.

I got up with the sunrise and finished cleaning up the kitchen. I took the trash out, and as I stood by the fence in the wet grass, I really wished I could see that deer again, just one more time.

Mom had changed. She couldn't talk, and her joints were so rigid her arms and legs were almost frozen in place. No one—not me, not William, not Cassandra, or the others, when they arrived—really knew what to do. Mom had soaked the bed, and I managed to get her into a fresh diaper. But changing her gown, the kind you pull over your head, was impossible because her arms were too stiff to bend. So I cut it off with shears, and called Marilyn, who was on her way to the airport. She had time for a detour.

Marilyn took my chin in her hand. "Your mother is entering what we call the *active dying phase*. Her old heart is just galloping along, trying to keep up. She will succumb in twenty-four to forty-eight hours." She let go of my chin.

Marilyn's certainty thudded off the floor, the walls, the ceiling. She showed me how to apply fentanyl patches for pain, how to record the frequency of dosage, and the importance of signing off on the paperwork, because, as usual—as you grapple with the vastness and profundity of it all—you have to fill out a form. I felt I had a lead straitjacket on. I couldn't move. I couldn't think. But I should have thought to ask, "What makes you think Mom will need painkillers?"

My cousins and siblings, the ones from far away, crowded onto the bed with Mom, and there wasn't room for me. I fought the urge to yell, "Get out!" because I still wanted Mom to myself. Instead I smiled at them, swallowed hard, and walked out.

Luanne, Daisy, and Murbeth sat in Mom's office, hunched over a pile of yellow, blue, and pink. Nightgowns—Daisy cut them up the back, so Mom's arms could get through the sleeves. Their heads bent over their careful, tiny stitches. I backed off, not wanting to intrude, and occupied myself with straightening the thirty or more crooked photographs lining the back hall. A picture of Mom in a school play, a picture of her sister with a huge white bow on her head, old-fashioned grandparents in pairs, dead uncles and aunts and cousins, group shots with ex-spouses who had never been heard from again. Walter and Cathy and her family were barely represented in Mom's collection.

Cassandra grabbed me from behind. "You need a manicure," she said, propelling me outside to the front steps. And as the day got hotter and hotter, she drove me crazy gluing flower decals on my bitten-down nails. "Hold still, girl!" she said. My hands were looking like a Latina teenager's. As she tried to get my foot in her lap to fix my toes, I ran for the kitchen.

The caterer, in a spotless green jacket, had appeared out of thin air with racks of wineglasses, coolers of food, and boxes of flowers for the big birthday party, which I had completely forgotten. But of course—like the wedding/funeral reception long ago—Death would again be offered a civilized luncheon, a cake, and a good stiff drink. We were cursed to do everything twice.

Compelled by the do-everything-twice curse, Cassandra bundled Mom up in a pink satin bathrobe and wheeled her out into the yard, where she sat at the table unable to talk, unable to eat, unable to drink, and hardly conscious, as we warbled through another round of "Happy Birthday" and ate another damn cake. When I die, please don't serve a cake with my name in yellow icing.

Finally, that day ended. All the guests returned to their respective motels except, somehow, William and me. We spent the night lying on either side of Mom, while dumb old Angela stretched out on the chaise longue, droning, "Any minute now," because Mom's breath rattled so slowly out of her, you just couldn't believe she was going to breathe back in. After a while we got used to the rhythm, like the waves at the beach, until at about 3 A.M., suddenly Mom landed in some kind of hell, howling, clawing at the bedclothes, pulling me to her chest with a supernatural force.

The pain patch I stuck on her chest had no effect so we stuck all the fentanyl on her at once. No relief. I dialed many phone numbers and got useless answering services. William and I ran around the house, shaking out toilet kits, digging through pockets, and when Sophie showed up, we commandeered her headache pills. Among us, we had two Percocets, three yellow Valiums, and a Tylenol, which we crushed, mixed with applesauce, and spooned into Mom's mouth, relieved that she could still swallow. Finally, she relaxed—until the stuff wore off and she went right back to thrashing and moaning. But we had nothing left.

In a last-ditch effort, I called the hospital, though I had little hope of any help. I kept getting transferred, put on hold, and transferred again. I was about to hang up when I got the geriatric resident and launched into my frantic plea. He cut me off. "No problem," he said. "What pharmacy can I phone this into for you?"

You could have blown me over. I jumped in the car and returned with a bucket of morphine, enough to sedate a hippo. That was the second miracle.

"Don't be scared," I said, and Mom opened her mouth eagerly for the dose, squeezing my fingers until they hurt. "Dying is so easy—everybody does it, Mom." Gradually her grip loosened and she sank deep into her body, barely getting from one breath to the next. Every so often, someone got up and squirted more morphine into her mouth. We were supposed to keep track on a form, but we didn't.

The long afternoon warped into night. My thirteen-year-old niece, bravely seeing death for the first time, was on her cell phone dispatching updates to her friends in L.A. from the other room. "She's, like, actually dying! My grandmother is, like, taking her last living breath here on earth!" The stuff the rest of us, with our age and maturity, could not say. Sisters, brothers, and cousins shifted from one spot to another on the bed, like the hands of a clock, taking breaks, returning, and regrouping.

I was cradling Mom's head when my eye strayed to the bedposts looming over us, the carved pineapples dark with age, their edges blunted by a century of polish. "You were born in this bed, weren't you, Mom?" I said, though I thought I was only thinking it. And right then she died. One second she was still deep down inside that husk of an old body and then—*pffft!* Gone. A little shift, like a blink.

It was the end. But it was not over.

I'd scripted this a billion times. I'd wash Mom with water, with sliced lemons in it—don't ask me where this came from. Then, after dressing her in yet another nightgown, I'd pack her room with flowers and leave her there on the bed for a while, until things kind of settled down.

Instead, *boom!* Everyone jumped up and went crazy, running around, making phone calls, closing windows, slamming doors, turning on the air-conditioning, which, it turned out, didn't work. Everyone was upset over a dead body that had been Mom a few minutes ago but now was this problem we had to dispose of.

William got squeamish, like Mom was going to rot on the spot, so he contacted the experts. But Black's funeral home needed a "pronouncement" from a qualified medical authority before they could touch the body—the body of Mom. We had no such authority, because we didn't get hospice.

"Call nine-one-one. The paramedics can do it," the man at the funeral parlor said. "Just make sure you don't get EMS."

"Who?"

"Emergency Medical Response. They can't pronounce. The paramedics can."

William called 911 and explained. Almost immediately, we heard the sirens. Five minutes later, the street was blocked off with trucks and cars, lights flashing. Neighbors emerged. An EMS team stormed the house like paratroopers. Three young women in navy-blue jumpsuits, straight out of EMS school, roared into the front hall with cables, computers, and black boxes that they were just dying to use, probably for the first time ever.

"We just need a pronouncement," I said, standing between my mother and this crazy anti-death squad. I had bare feet; they had big black boots. The leader with the blond ponytail and clipboard barked, "I don't have time for this." She pushed me out of the way, charging into Mother's room.

Sophie and Cassandra, dignified and solemn, looked up from the body, a basin of lemon slices and water between them on the bed, while my niece delivered a blow-by-blow commentary to the West Coast. "She's dead! Grandmother will never walk the earth again!"

"Clear out," the blonde said to them, lifting my mother's eyelids and feeling her neck. Another knelt on the floor and whipped out a portable defibrillator, powering it up. In my mind's eye, I saw Mom's corpse jerking on the bed. It had taken her so long to die, and she had wanted to so badly. I was in the absurd position of preventing my mother from being revived or, as I saw it, defiled.

"Stop! I have a 'Do Not Resuscitate' right here," I said, waving six pages of fine print in the team captain's face. "Right here. 'Do Not Resuscitate.' Very legal. DNR. Put the paddles back in the box and get off my Mom."

"You are interfering with the law," said the blonde angrily.

"So arrest me," I said, pointing to the door. "Out there."

I backed the EMS team out of Mom's room and we stood in the dim hallway, the boss girl speed-reading my DNR.

"This is no good," said the blond woman, tossing the papers in my face and gesturing her team back in. I stood in their way, all ninety-nine pounds of me. I noticed the handcuffs swinging on the bossy one's belt.

Two policemen barged in, the screen door slamming behind them. They had guns and clubs. I handed the papers to the older cop, who might have more sense than these teenagers. "This legal and fully legitimate document clearly indicates that my mother did not want to be resuscitated."

"Do you have any more copies?" He asked.

"No," I lied. With only one document, six pages long, I figured it would take them a while to read it if they had to pass it around. He paged through the fine print. "You need a 'Do Not Resuscitate' order signed by two doctors and notarized," the cop told me.

"I'm from Canada. I didn't know."

He looked at his watch. "Where are the paramedics?" he asked the blond lady, who was about to explode.

"Look, they're in Passaic. Might get here in five minutes. I could lose my job if I don't get to procedure."

I stepped toward them and played the sympathy card.

"Help me. My mother died an hour ago. She wanted to die. She did not want to be revived."

"Let me see that," the other cop said. He began to read the faulty document that I produced. He read it slowly, his lips moving, his finger inching along each line. The magic sympathy card had worked. He was on my side, stalling for time. He questioned me: When did your mother have a stroke? When did she come home from the hospital? When did she die? Why didn't you have a doctor on call? I answered very slowly.

"I'm leaving," the EMS lady screamed. "I will not be responsible for this!" And she stomped off into the night, her fellow EMS workers following. But the woman carrying the defibrillator stopped on the way out and touched my shoulder. "Sorry for your loss."

I almost didn't know what she was talking about. I hadn't had a chance to experience my loss.

Finally, the paramedics showed up, looked at my papers, and said cheerfully, "Those are just fine, ma'am." A young man with a soul patch and a stethoscope actually grinned at me. "Where's the deceased at?" The third miracle.

Mom had now been dead for hours. While the paramedics legally established this rather obvious fact, I sat with the policemen in the kitchen and was lectured on procedure in the State of New Jersey.

"See, if you decided to sue? We could all lose our jobs."

I cared about their jobs right now? My mother was dead. I wanted to help wash and dress her. I wanted to touch her hands. I wanted to cry.

"I live in another country, for Christ's sake. We have all this great legal-looking paper. How was I supposed to know ahead of time that this documentation is insufficient? How was I supposed to know that my mother would die at home? In Nova Scotia, you don't need a document to die."

"That's Canada for you. Around here, we don't want to get sued—and we don't want to charge you with murder, either."

It was 1 A.M. I offered them doughnuts and opened a can of beer. As I held the door to let them out, two little old men in wrinkled black suits arrived from Black's funeral home. They were so frail, I was afraid they'd faint if they did anything more than sit down for a cup of tea. But the old men wrestled mom's body into a black plastic bag and zippered it up. With an absolute minimum of dialogue, they got the paperwork out of the way and went bumping down the front-door steps to the hearse. I never did get my moment with Mom.

As a result of this little drama, I plan to get DNR tattooed on my chest in big blue letters, just below the clavicle, where you can't miss it, along with my lawyer's name and phone number. Because, frankly, nothing stands between you and a return trip from the grave but the right paperwork, and if you can't find it when you need it, you are totally out of luck.

In the days after my mother died, Cassandra and I stayed in the house because we didn't want to leave. I had lost my mother. Cassandra had lost her job and her friend. "In my country, when people get angry, they fight. They cut and kill each other all the time. The cops only come after someone is dead, not to break up the fight. But your mother, when she was angry, she turned the other cheek. I learned a lot from her. That was something new to me." Then Cassandra laughed. "Ha, ha. Unless she was really mad!"

Wandering through the house, I threw a bunch of withered zinnias and marigolds into the trash and straightened the cushions on the fresh new TV-room sofa that had just arrived. Many pairs of Mother's reading glasses were sprinkled about the house, though they were just props, like the open books she liked to hold. Sunlight and blue shadows crossed the floor, and the light outside shimmered in the oaks that lined the backyard. Closing a book she would not open again, washing her lipstick off a glass, I felt Mother's absence.

Cassandra and I waxed furniture, vacuumed rugs, and washed towels. We washed the windows twice. We sorted my mother's clothes, gave some away, and threw some out. "Her old shoe," Cassandra said, holding one out. I took it in my hands. Unless she was all dressed up and wanted Pappagallos, Mother would wear only the dilapidated old blue suede ones. They were worn straight through, the heels nonexistent, and the leather at the toes rumpled. As with so many things, there was nothing to do except throw them away.

The house had never been so clean or so empty, and finally we ran out of stuff to do.

Black's funeral home called to ask me about Mom's clothes and hairdo. "Cassandra, was Mom still going to that hairdresser at the Colony?"

"No. I do it."

"You've been fixing her hair? It's the funeral home. You want to do it now?"

Cassandra jumped up, grabbed the car keys, and was out the door. "You don't know how to get there!" I called after her. She forgot Mom's pink Chanel suit and had to come back for it.

Two hours later, she returned. She threw her bag on the counter and dropped onto a chair at the table. "I need a drink," she said. Cassandra never drank.

"All we have is wine and scotch."

"Gimme some of that scotch. A big glass." She looked totally rattled.

It turned out that Cassandra had never been around a dead body before. She'd seen people die in the line of duty at nursing homes, but she had never fixed a hairdo for a dead person. "You had to jump in with both feet, didn't you?" I said.

She nodded her head five times.

"And I dressed her, too. You should have seen that funny little man. Same as what picked her up? Oh, I had a good time with him. We talked to your mother. I said 'Now, Addie, I am putting on your slip. Now, Addie, I am putting on your blouse.' "

"As long as she didn't talk back."

Cassandra laughed. "She looks good."

"Oh, don't tell me that. I hate that, when people say how great dead people look."

"Well, she does."

"Then what is the point of living?" I asked, and poured her another drink.

We wound up with a viewing prior to the cremation. Though Mom told me she wanted to donate her body to science, I kept my mouth shut. Besides, I wasn't sure that science would actually want it. She'd said many things to many people. And as Roland pointed out, there was no reason to entertain the validity of any final unwritten wishes—unless you wanted to walk naked through a briar patch.

My mother, laid out in the rental coffin they display you in if you are being cremated, looked pretty made over. Her face, serene and all plumped up with embalming fluid, practically glowed with artificial health. Cassandra had done a very faithful makeup job and managed to get gloves on Mother's dead hands. How, I can't imagine. Mom, framed by white ruffles, was centered in the middle of three adjoining rooms that had the look and feel of a living room stage set.

The place was packed. People of all races, ages, and sizes clomped up the central staircase and flooded the rooms, crowding the couches and armchairs, and ignoring the deceased after a brief acknowledgment. No one tells you how to act at these things, so people revert to their default personas—the country club, the office party, the family gathering.

"She taught me to read," said Lorna, a middle-aged woman with three kids at home. "If it wasn't for your mother, I'd still be cleaning houses." Lorna now had an office job with benefits.

"Your mother visited my mother every week for a year, until she died," said another: Mom's hospice work, something that had ended when Walter showed up on the scene. Another woman was so overcome she couldn't speak; Mom had bought her a house after her family fell on hard times. I was touched and very proud of her, but the litany of good works began to sound like a public-relations campaign. To one misty-eyed man, I almost replied, "Yes, I've always been so grateful to Mother for teaching me life's finer skills, like how to drink and drive."

An ancient, bent-over black lady with a Tina Turner wig shuffled up to me and said, "You know, I've always loved your mother." She dabbed her eyes with a cloth hanky. "Edith was a burning light of God." Clearly she didn't know my mother. Perhaps mourning was her hobby. She smiled at me and said, "Why, her scarf even matches the drapes! Did you plan that?" I looked around. There were no drapes.

Before I could muster a reply to this remarkable observation, Walter made an entrance, and a hush fell over the proceedings. Wheeled in by Cathy, he looked peachy, pink-cheeked, and relaxed in a yellow polo shirt and khakis. "What's all this?" I heard him ask.

"This is Addie's wake, Dad," said Cathy.

"Ah, so," said Walter. Cathy wheeled Walter up to the coffin, where vague confusion passed over his face. "Why is that woman asleep at this party?" he asked. Cathy, looking unbearably sad, wheeled him away. Walter didn't recognize his Bride. He didn't know she was dead. In fact, he seemed to have forgotten her altogether. His week in the hospital had erased his life with my mother.

That afternoon, in accordance with Mother's will, Walter moved back into the house, and I moved out, into the tattered arms of the Devonshire Inn, never to sleep in Mother's house again.

The morning before Mom's memorial service, William and I got up early and drove out to the crematorium in the Ferngrove Cemetery. We drove past the house Mother was born in, the house she grew up in, the house she lived in when she married my father and where William grew up, and the house across the street, where I was raised. With its ancient beech trees and swimming pool, it was the last house she lived in before Dad died. Mom had lived her whole life within three square miles.

An August heat was coming on, and cicadas twanged and buzzed high up in the trees against an unbearably blue sky. No one else came to the cremation, satisfied to attend the memorial service later in the day. "Well, I figured I was onboard for the tour," William said. I felt the same. He and I had started this crazy journey with Mom, and we would see it through to the end.

Ferngrove is an old resting place, dating back to the Civil War.

The scale and grandeur of its monuments and crypts are from a gilded age when the one good thing about dying was the trip to glory to follow. But few descendants remain above ground to maintain the memory of the dead buried below, and the place has become a bit seedy. I doubt the crematorium was part of the original plan, the smokestack baldly indicating a rather crude, if reliable, means of ascent. My maternal grandparents rest in a neglected shrine barely visible in the shadows of an overgrown hemlock.

A cluster of low brick buildings stood to one side. Behind them rose a mountain of wood chips. A backhoe dumped a load of dead flowers into an industrial-size Dumpster, and the smell of compost and diesel fumes blew toward me. The glass doors were unlocked, so we wandered in through a small auditorium adorned with fake flowers and powder-blue wall-to-wall carpeting. White plastic chairs stood abandoned in crooked rows, as though abruptly vacated. "Eternal Life" leaflets were scattered on the floor. It was devastating.

We kept walking and found ourselves outside again, in a small overgrown rose garden, poorly tended, the legacy of some family that had died out decades ago. Though in need of pruning, the graveyard roses were spectacular. Red Floribunda, Pink Dawn, and the yellow and pink blush of the Peace rose, named for Armistice Day, Dad's favorite. He'd been dead for nearly nineteen years, and I smiled when I thought of him. Someday I'd smile when I thought of my mother, but not just yet.

Wandering through the garden, we came to a garage that turned out to be the actual crematorium. The place was shopworn, not dirty, but darkened from years of blast-furnace temperatures. There were a few windows in one wall, and a floor-to-ceiling bank of ovens in the opposite wall. A man in gray overalls was fiddling with some dials on the side of an oven. Popping up out of nowhere and utterly out of place, William and I unnerved him. "Wouldn't you like to sit in the chapel, the Meditation Room?" he inquired. "Before the, er, ah . . ."

"If you don't mind, we'd rather wait here," William said. The stripped-down, utilitarian workroom was a relief after the creepy Meditation Room with its "celebration of life" motif. My mother was dead.

A hearse backed into the oven room. One of the wrinkled old men from Black's funeral home emerged and hauled out a large cardboard box, like an oversize FedEx package, with the word HEAD written across the top in Magic Marker. We had reached the point where the burden of euphemism was abandoned.

With a look of practiced sympathy, the old man slid my mother in her box onto a rickety metal gurney. He offered each of us a rose to put on the lid, a totally sappy gesture I could not resist. William, his hands shaking, followed suit.

"There's no wire in those? No plastic?" the oven man asked.

"Nope, they can go right in," said the old man.

The oven man said, "The plastic lumps up, see." And who wants plastic lumps mixed in with their loved one?

The flowers thudded on the box, revealing, like some sort of sonar, an aural image of Mother's body inside. I wondered if she was naked or clothed—because the buttons on her pink Chanel suit were definitely plastic.

"How hot is the oven?" I asked the overalls man.

"About two thousand degrees." He couldn't help but look a little pleased about being an expert on the subject.

"How long does it take?"

"Three to five hours, depending on the size of the person."

"How do you know when it's done?"

"I look." He gestured, and I saw that each oven had a small Pyrex window slot.

The oven man rolled the gurney along the uneven floor. We walked with him, accompanying Mom on either side, and watched as he winched the cardboard box up to the top oven rack, opened the door, and with a metal rod, pushed it in. Then the door banged shut.

This was his job. This dark metal room with its roaring flames and cooling ashes was his ordinary, everyday work. He pushed a button and you could hear the flames come up, just like a gas barbecue. The whole thing was kitchen-like, oddly domestic and familiar. It wasn't so bad. We stood for a few minutes, listening. And then we left, arm in arm.

EPILOGUE

When my book found a publisher, my very first impulse was to tell Addie. I forgot she was dead, and that a book exposing her most compromising experiences would hardly have made her happy.

But now that her life is over and mine goes on, I often imagine having lunch with her at the Oldhill Golf Club (an event I dreaded in real life). We sit in the warm summer sun, on the flagstone terrace with a view of the greens, hazy in the heavy air, the *poc-poc* from the tennis courts in the background.

Fully restored, she is resplendent in her white linen suit with the black collar and cuffs, her black sling-backs showing off her great legs. She's wearing her sapphire ring—and I'm wearing it, too, the ring I can never lose. With her beautiful dappled tan, her eyes are twice as blue, framed by the brim of her black straw hat.

"That color looks well on you, dear," Addie says, giving my pink floral shirtdress the once-over. My friends would die laughing. I never wore my normal clothing—jeans, boots, ribbed sweaters, tank tops, sandals—when I visited Oldhill. I kept a special wardrobe just for her. I thought everybody did so to please their moms.

She looks approvingly at the white-coated waiters, the green-and-white golf-club china, and the hanging baskets of fuchsias and petunias dangling from the beams.

"I think I'll have a cocktail, Meggo. How's about you?" Her eyes twinkle.

I gave up drinking in real life, but all things being equal, I think I'll join her. Addie, with a friendly, authoritative gesture, beckons a waiter. "I'll have a double vodka on the rocks, and my daughter will have a dry martini—no Tanqueray? Then Beefeater. You like yours straight up, don't you, dear?" Yes, I do, because from my perspective, ice cubes just get in the way.

Addie fusses with the packet of breadsticks on the table, extracting one and spearing bits of butter with it. Addie'd be perfectly happy dispensing with the breadstick all together and just eating the butter. She waves off a yellow jacket with her napkin, to no avail.

"Well, here's to your success," she says. "But you were pretty hard on me."

"Mom, I didn't say anything that wasn't true."

"No, but you left out the fact that in my day, you could buy restraining sheets for babies at the department store. And I didn't have the sage advice of any child psychologist. Children were to be trained and molded—and if that meant tying them to the bed for their own good, we did it." Mom sniffs a little defensively and fans the persistent yellow jacket away.

"Wasps find me irresistible," she says.

"But, Mom! What about the clothesline?"

"Well, clearly, restraining sheets didn't work on you. And a little clothesline might have helped your children sleep through the night. Then you wouldn't have been such a wreck."

My Italian husband encouraged our three children to sleep in our bed. No clothesline for him! I don't know why we bothered with a three-bedroom house when we could have lived in a studio apartment.

"Tell me about your job," Addie says. "What are you up to now, darling?"

I take a breath, because Addie isn't going to like this. "I'm sticking around the house these days, Mom." Addie abruptly looks away and sips her vodka. She is visualizing me in a chenille bathrobe, shuffling around with a coffee mug, nothing she can be proud of.

"But surely the children don't need you, not at their age!"

Of course, my teenagers would *say* they didn't. But, whether they'd say so or not, right now, I'm happy to stay put, fiddling with my writing at the kitchen table. I want them to know they can saunter by, pretending to ignore me, anytime they want.

I smile, but I don't say a word until she stops giving me her penetrating look and changes the topic.

"And how is that dear husband of yours?" Addie is not asking about Rob; she's asking about *us*.

"We'll be married twenty-five years in October. And we get along fine." I don't even add, *ever since you died, Mom.* Had Addie lived a year longer, our little family unit would not have survived the stress of my commutes, and I'd be in a mental institution.

Addie sighs. "Well, I've always said the second twenty years are so much easier than the first twenty."

I'd heard these encouraging words many times. But when your idea of "going to bed" is going to sleep because you are perpetually exhausted, the promise of happiness in twenty years is not much comfort.

"That was certainly true of your father and me," Addie continues, rattling the ice cubes around in her glass. "We were married for forty years." She pauses, having a new thought. "Perhaps that was the real problem with Walter."

"What?"

Addie looks at me earnestly. "We just weren't married long enough."

A breeze stirs the pines at the edge of the verandah, ruffles the tablecloth, and shivers the stand of maples. A few clouds gather past the eighteenth hole, promising rain. But for now, the perfect yellow summer sun gilds everything.

"I'm starving!" Addie says, avidly opening her menu. "Look, they have that wonderful Cobb salad! Or maybe the shrimp?" She makes a little gleeful face. "What are you going to order?"

The club sandwich is a reliable old standby, but I always find that extra slice of bread in the middle overwhelming. "Grilled cheese, in honor of Dad," I say. My father loved a nice grilled cheese sandwich. Mom nods with approval.

"What a good choice," she says, raising her glass, a half-moon of lipstick on the rim. "Here's to you, dear." Addie smiles tenderly, right at me. "Enjoy your life!"

Acknowledgments

I am grateful to many kind and insightful professionals, friends, and relatives over the course of ten years:

My agents, Carolyn Swayze and Kris Rothstein, at the Carolyn Swayze Literary Agency; Susan Mercandetti, Millicent Bennett, Abigail Presser, Janet Wygal, and a host of others at Random House; Nancy Meinerstagen, who pushed me through the first draft; Helen Berliner, my co-conspirator, who read every word aloud and dry-cleaned the manuscript; Jim Gimian, Joe Spieler, Sheilagh McEvenue, and, from way back, Andy Pedersen.

Margot Horsey took each step with me *and* my mother; Julie Chender listened to every detail; Heather Rose, Ellen Sherlock, Leslie Patten, Beth Polous, Paula Yanch are all precious friends; Barb and Paul were steady at the corner store.

To my brothers and sisters, nieces and nephews, cousins, and my stepsister, who shared these experiences, if not exactly my view of them; my three excellent children—who raised *me*—and to good old Rob, who endures; Mabel and Pauline—to whom I owe a debt of love, and thanks for all that jam.

To the dedicated staff at the Departure Lounge, who made each day possible.

To Douglas Penick, who shows me the way because he is ahead of me.

To Chogyam Trungpa, Rinpoche and Dzongzar Khyentse, Rinpoche—the light in the dark.

About the Author

MEG FEDERICO regularly writes humor for the *National Post*. Her work has appeared in *The Globe and Mail, Shambhala Sun, Agni Magazine,* and on CBC Radio. She is a palliative-care volunteer and also works with VON's Breakaway Adult Day Program. She lives in Halifax with her family.

About the Type

This book was set in Sabon, a typeface designed by the well-known German typographer Jan Tschichold (1902–74). Sabon's design is based upon the original letter forms of Claude Garamond and was created specifically to be used for three sources: foundry type for hand composition, Linotype, and Monotype. Tschichold named his typeface for the famous Frankfurt typefounder Jacques Sabon, who died in 1580.